THE
FISHING
DETECTIVE

THE
FISHING
DETECTIVE

A New Approach to Coarse Angling

JOHN BAILEY

St Michael

FROM

MARKS & SPENCER

First published in 1994 by
Collins Willow
an imprint of HarperCollins*Publishers*
London

This edition published specially for Marks & Spencer in 1996
by HarperCollins*Publishers*, London

© John Bailey 1994

A CIP catalogue for this book
is available from the British Library

ISBN 0 583 32454 1

Photographs by John Bailey
Illustrations by Paul Groombridge

Printed and bound in Italy

CONTENTS

A very fine young angler, Richard Slater from Northampton, studies a water completely new to him. Wisely, he was in no hurry to fish and spent a good hour quietly walking the banks of the lake before making a decision that proved very worthwhile, for it resulted in his biggest-ever crucian carp.

INTRODUCTION

A very instructive story is told about Richard Walker, the great father of angling in this century. Walker had been requested to make a television programme about barbel fishing. This was in the early days of the small screen and television camerawork was in its infancy, so Walker had to catch the barbel in full daylight – quite a problem in itself. What made the producer and cameraman even more worried was the fact that the master spent the first half of the day not fishing at all but simply looking at the river. Up and down he strolled, looking, thinking and not saying a word. This, just to compound everyone's problems, was the first time he had ever set foot on those banks!

By now the TV team was tearing out its collective hair, but at last Walker took out a rod and cast his first bait into the river. The story goes that the bait was a worm, a natural bait that Walker knew would be instantly acceptable should a barbel be there. A barbel was there and the worm was instantly accepted! Within sixty seconds of Walker's beginning to fish the cameras were rolling and two of three minutes after that a beautiful specimen was on the bank. It was a wrap! From dejection the mood turned to exhilaration and the entire crew were in the pub before closing time, celebrating a true fishing detective!

The moral is plain for all to see. The successful angler will not jump in but use every single weapon at his disposal – most vitally his eyes, his brain and his deductive powers. Before we go any further, I must stress the fact that every water, every fish and every little event at the bankside tells its own story. Nothing happens by chance but is rather one link in a whole chain of events that can be unravelled if the time is taken to stop and ponder. There is, for the angling detective, always something to watch, to consider and to understand. This – for me anyway and soon I hope for you – is the true magic of angling. Even if you catch nothing, no day is ever really a blank, for something can

be observed, understood and mentally or otherwise noted for future reference.

The purpose of this book is to help you interpret the evidence that is available from any typical angling session. I stress the word 'typical'. I do some diving and a little underwater photography and I could have employed some of these pictures to give, perhaps, more drama, but what would have been the point? Probably only one angler in a thousand has access to this sort of gear and so any underwater shots would really only be the stuff of fantasy. The whole point is that the experiences recounted and the lessons drawn here can be shared and added to by every single reader. For this reason I have only photographed, illustrated and written what anybody else can see for themselves and in this way I hope I have made my message truly accessible.

Let me stress that, as I see it, the vital aspect of this book is not merely gathering evidence at the waterside but rather linking it to the solution of problems. Everywhere there are clues which, if read correctly, help catch more fish, often radically improving previous catch rates. The term 'watercraft' describes some of what I have mentioned so far. Everybody who fishes for a while develops watercraft, which in reality is just a feel for the water that is acquired as your fishing experience grows. But watercraft is often simply a subconscious development and can be a vague feeling that is often ignored or at least not further investigated. To be a fishing detective calls for harder, more positive work, more careful thought and, not least, the all-important ability to translate sightings of fish into fish on the bank.

Let me say at the start that this book will not always be right all the time on every water that you fish. This is the beauty of angling: because it is linked to nature, it cannot be totally predictable. Hopefully there will be times when you will raise your eyebrows over what I

Above: The Wye was very clear on this August day and exactly the right approach was to cast out as far as possible so that a bait could be trotted with the current in a natural-looking fashion. In conditions like this a static bait will often be rejected in favour of something moving and smaller.

Left: Wolterton Lake, in Norfolk, was at one time home to many very large tench. Then something happened: the fish all but disappeared and a bite was an event to be noted. To this day nobody really knows the reason. But that does not stop many well-known local anglers from visiting the water repeatedly to monitor its progress. The hope is that one of these days the 'Marsh', as we still like to call it, will return to its former glory and perhaps the malaise that has affected it for so many years will be understood.

have written and strongly disagree. We are dealing with nature, and there will always be alternative deductions to be made from the clues that she gives out. A fishing detective is always aware, always thinking, and never dismisses out of hand any clue he may be lucky enough to be given. The essential thing to realize is that as long as you are watching, listening and thinking, your catch rate is bound to rise.

The popular image of the angler is of a fat man, possibly a little drunk, asleep in the afternoon sunshine with a string tied to his big toe in the hope that some plump, obliging fish comes along and hooks itself. This image is just about as far from the fishing detective as it is possible to be. Of course, it is possible to cast two baits to the horizon and settle down for a weekend's sleep in a bivvy but where is the fun, the excitement or the satisfaction in that? Read this book, think about it and most important of all put it to the test, and then

see if you don't agree with me.

To my mind, the finest fisherman and naturalist of this and probably any other century is Hugh Falkus. Hugh has that rare gift of being able to make the most complex angling considerations accessible and attractive and it was he and his writings above everything that made me realize how much more there is to fishing than simply sitting on a bank, under an umbrella, blind to the world about you.

Some words of Hugh's in particular, which I first read over fifteen years ago, made an everlasting impression on me: 'We must learn to use our eyes in a new way – or rather, in a very old way: the way of our ancestral hunters. By giving ourselves a chance to flex those hidden hunting instincts, which, like wizened muscles, have been inhibited by centuries of urban life, we begin to sharpen our powers of observation and deduction. From this growing consciousness of what is really happening in nature, we start to see and to understand a host of things we have never before even noticed. And then, suddenly, like Alice through her looking glass, we find we have stepped into a strange and wonderful new world where nothing is ever quite the same again.'

It was after reading those words that I stopped and thought about what I had been doing throughout my fishing career, which had begun in the mid 1950s. I had always marvelled at what I had seen at the waterside and Hugh's words crystallized everything for me: fishing is a wonderful reason and excuse to turn back the clock, to retrace our steps to a hunting, predatorial

past before life was cosy and secure. To be an angling detective is to be totally at one with nature.

Like our hunting ancestors, the fishing detective needs to use his eyes and his common sense to interpret what he sees going on around him. Let us look at some simple examples. Suppose a grebe continually dives into the same area of water, or the gulls circle it, or a cormorant is seen snaking sinuously around the same stretch of water, then what does the detective deduce? Obviously fish are in residence there, and probably packed up tightly in great numbers. Nothing very surprising about that. But, supposing the fish are small, then it is probable that underwater predators

It is the summer of 1993 and I am hard at work photographing some carp in an arm of a very weedy water. It is surprising how effective a long camera lens can be for fish watching. Even if you do not always take photographs, you can still use it to magnify fish as if you were watching them at very close range A tripod is nearly always necessary to avoid camera shake. Incidentally, pale clothing, which is much more comfortable in hot weather, poses no problem in detective work as it does not stand out as much as many anglers think. This is probably because the fish are looking up at you and see you silhouetted against the sky so that you appear as a black shape whatever the colour of what you are wearing.

Fishing detection is not always an intense business. This photograph was taken after two Frenchmen had spent the period around dawn showing me barbel lies up and down the river and talking in a relaxed way about the depths and the current speeds. Once the sun was up, however, they assured me that the barbel would go back to sleep and the best thing was to have a celebratory glass of red wine or two to commemorate the capture of a 6lb fish and the cementing of Anglo-French relations.

Left: Children often make the best detectives – not as I have heard it suggested, because their size makes them less obvious to the fish, but because they have more time, sometimes more patience and are happier to watch and listen than adults, who usually seem to be in a hurry to achieve concrete results. These keen-eyed children had seen two good-sized perch go by, which I found very interesting because I did not know perch had come back to the Bure. This shot was taken at an interesting site where every so often shoals of large bream or the occasional huge roach passes underneath the bridge. Over a few days of careful watching it is possible to build up a useful picture of fish movements, sizes and habits.

will have gathered just as surely as feathered ones, and perch or pike could very well be in hungry attendance in the same area.

Now let us imagine a coot swimming over open water, entirely alone. Suddenly, it rears up, angry, feathers out, treading the water noisily. This continues for half a minute before the bird settles down and continues on its way. Almost certainly it will have seen something in the water to have frightened it. The pike

angler needs no further encouragement.

The fishing detective will need to be a botanist as well as a naturalist. For example, he will learn that the true bulrush tends to grow only on a hard bottom, preferably over gravel, a fact that is not lost on the tench population of a lake. Likewise he will begin to know which waterweeds grow at which depths and by just looking over a lake he will be able to form a quick but accurate impression of depth ranges.

Just like his distant ancestors, the fishing detective will also become an expert reader of the weather. Even without modern satellite forecasts, he will begin to recognize the cloud formations that herald the approach of a depression – something that in itself can switch off feeding fish completely. Alternatively, in the winter, he may begin to notice a different cloud formation after midday which could lead to a totally clear and starry sky at night. Ally this with a moon and a total absence of any breeze and he knows a hard frost is bound to fall, with all its various consequences for the following day's sport.

The fishing detective does, however, have many

The cormorant is the one water bird about which I have very severe reservations, for the amount of fish that it can eat is phenomenal. Very often cormorants will settle on a lake throughout the winter in great numbers and virtually denude it of fish. This happened at Norfolk's Holkham Hall lake in the early 1960s: what had been an extraordinarily vital environment was by 1968 almost barren of fish, largely thanks to these voracious birds. Having witnessed two cormorants enter a trout stewpond, I can testify that the destruction they can wreak in such confined areas can only be compared to the damage foxes do in hen-houses.

I have to thank the excellent Danish photographer and fisherman Johnny Jensen for this fine shot of a coot we both saw when pike fishing a Norfolk lake. The bird was making its way across a relatively deep, sheltered bay when this disturbance broke out. A short time later we saw a sizeable pike hunting in the bay and a long cast resulted in a fourteen-pounder which fell to livebait.

advantages over his prehistoric counterpart. In the Stone Age, Polaroid glasses were not available. Nor were there binoculars or echo sounders and certainly not inflatable boats or even virtually indestructible canoes. Neither was there the vast range of water-proof and warm clothing now available to make the art of fishing and fish detection so much more enjoy-able, so much less painful. Here, then, is the key: the fishing detective resurrects all the old skills and instincts dormant in modern man and supplements them with all the benefits of modern technology. Provided he is ever thoughtful and conscientious in what he does, the final result should be almost total efficiency. I say 'almost' advisedly, for the simple reason that nature will never be fully understood – and, fortunately, far less tamed.

The morning sunshine of the tail end of November highlights a hopeful bream angler. The night had been clear and cold, a fact which obviously would work against any success with that species, but cloud was beginning to well up from the south-west and the wind was steadily strengthening. I would definitely share our angler's optimism that this change in the weather and softening of the light and temperature could bring a shoal onto the feed.

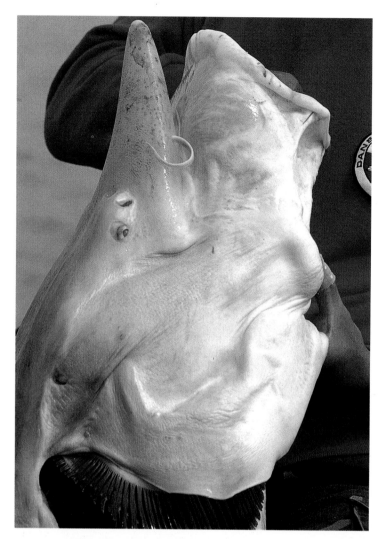

Left: That bible of all young anglers back in the 1950s, the Observer's Book of Freshwater Fishes, says that the sturgeon feeds by 'routing about in the mud and the sand of the sea bed with its long snout for mud-loving organisms. The mud is sucked into the mouth, the edible matter retained and the unwanted material afterwards spat out.' For this reason, many British anglers grew up believing that these impressive fish were virtually uncatchable. This is far from true, however, and that huge mouth telescopes out to suck in very large live fish which it crushes with huge throat teeth. So, never take received wisdom about fish behaviour totally on trust, for anglers' detective work is constantly revising the picture.

Below: Carp deepen in colour in winter, to the extent that you can always identify a winter-caught fish in a photograph, even without a background of bare trees or dead rushes to give you a clue.

WITNESS

The general condition of the fish, its overall shape and the presence of wounds or identifying marks, all play an important part in helping the angler recognize or classify a specimen. Talking of marks, wounds do take a long time to heal. I knew of some barbel caught once in 1990 and kept in nets until many of the dorsal fins split. These fins still had not healed by autumn 1993. I contacted a shoal of bream in 1980 and a decade afterwards in 1990. Two members bore recognizable pike scars even though a decade separated the captures. The moral is to treat fish with respect, for their bodies cry shame long afterwards if we do not.

A fish's physical characteristics accurately reflect and bear witness to the nature of its environment and its lifestyle. There is a lot to learn from the body of a fish without having to resort to scale reading, post-mortems or anything too scientific.

Photographic evidence

What follows is a series of photographic portraits of fish from which several important deductions can be made. Let us start with a dramatic example: the head of a beluga sturgeon. Now, I was brought up to believe that sturgeon were virtually uncatchable and lived off microscopic creatures in the mud. When I was a child this was the heresy spread by books about fish. Look at the photograph top left, showing that enormous telescopic mouth. Why would nature create such a funnel if the only things to go down it were creatures smaller than a pea? The old books were wrong, for in fact that mouth often swallows a carp of 5lb or even double that weight.

Look at the winter-caught carp shown opposite. It is a beautiful colour, with excellent fins and no damage to it at all, and is also quite a big fish at just over 16lb. But note the lack of depth between the pectoral and ventral fins. The fish is shaped really more like a tench or a barbel without any of the pot-bellied depth you often see in mirror and leather carp. The reason for this is that it was caught from a very shallow estate lake and all the fish have grown long and lean to accommodate the lack of depth. This affects them in no way at all apart from weight. They live and grow long and are clearly healthy. But the angler wanting a thirty-pounder would be wise to move on.

Variations in carp

The lateral mirror carp seen at the top of page 16 is a totally different beast from the winter-caught leather. It was caught from a deep, food-rich pit where it has very little competition indeed. The fish in fact is only around four years old (perhaps even a little less) and already it weighs nearly 9lb. For me, fish this shape lack grace and dignity but there is no doubt that if it is size you are after this will be the type of water for you.

The middle fish on page 16 is almost certainly a true wild carp. How can you tell? A very good question and even the experts can often be confused. First, you have to be fairly sure that the water has had no stockings for many, many years, and this water certainly has remained untouched. Secondly, just look at the shape of the fish itself – long, torpedo-like and without any build-up of muscle on the shoulders or flab on the stomach. Next have a look at the colour: you will notice that the fish is no more than tinged with gold and is quite pale overall. This is typical of the wildie, a sub-species that rarely shows dramatic coloration. I would put my money on this 6lb fish being a wildie.

Compare the obvious common seen at the bottom of page 16 with the wildie. First, you will see that this fish is much more rotund, and has a bigger back and a more bulging stomach. Secondly, you will notice that the colours are much more vivid and brassy. Also, I know that the lake in question was stocked with mirrors and commons some twenty years ago and there is no way that this can be a wildie.

GONE MISSING

One of the great wildlife tragedies of recent decades has been the dramatic decline of the dashing, boldly coloured rudd right across England and Wales.

What happened during the 1960s and 1970s was that former rudd strongholds became populated with mirror carp populations. By comparison, rudd are a gentle, retiring species and in many cases they have been swamped and ultimately wiped out by the bigger foreign invaders. Just as serious is the large number of rudd ponds and lakes that have dried up as a result of increased water abstraction or drought, or have been filled in to provide more land for housing or industry. All in all, the prospects for rudd in Britain are probably worse now than they have ever been since the Ice Age receded and coarse fish populations began to become established.

The only recourse is to seek out waters that have been forgotten or have escaped the eagle eye of the planners or the fishery committee, intent on stocking Italian mirror carp. Such waters might be long-neglected farm ponds or lakes tucked away in the middle of country estates. Parts of mid Wales, the deep West Country, and Norfolk and Suffolk still offer some sanctuary to rudd shoals simply because they are relatively tucked away.

In my search for rudd waters, one interesting piece of evidence has emerged: it seems that rudd are quite resistant to salt in their environment and some excellent rudd habitats have appeared in coastal dykes and drains, especially down the eastern side of the country from Lincolnshire to Essex and centred on Suffolk. Many of these environments were created as dykes to drain land and to turn it into fields for agricultural purposes. For decades they have largely been ignored by anglers and considered only fit for eels and flounders. This is a mistake. Often, even within earshot of the roaring sea, rudd flash and dart beneath blue skies, along waters flanked by corn fields.

As far as I know, this is the most northerly water in the British Isles to hold rudd. They most likely came here in livebait cans, brought by pike fishermen and deposited at the end of the day. The strange thing is that they have grown very large and there have even been rumours of one four-pounder. This I find hard to believe, however, for we are talking about a water not far south of Inverness. But stranger things have happened and certainly decent tench are present here.

The photograph above is really one of the most beautiful shots of a barbel I have ever seen and every aspect of it tells its own tale. Look at the sharp, pointed nose, capped with a muscle-like gristle – ideal for digging into the gravel, dislodging a stone or rooting under weed. Then look at the four barbules that surround its mouth. These are like fingertips and they can slide into the gravel and detect the presence of, for example, caddis grubs, and all other types of food. Watch a barbel at close quarters and you will see just how much it relies on these little fingers of flesh. Now look at the barbel's large underslung mouth nestling between the barbules. The positioning is perfect for a fish that glides back and forth over the bottom, hoovering in food as it goes The lips can be extended, to act like a small vacuum cleaner, sucking in items of food from some distance.

Streamlined design

Note the general shape of the fish – long and streamlined with a slight hump above the head and around the shoulders and a flattish stomach. When a barbel becomes big it just fills out and grows still heavier shoulders rather than putting weight on the belly. This leanness is clearly important in helping the fish to hug the gravel bed in a fast current.

Let us move on now to the picture on the left of Joy holding a small French barbel. It is small but beautiful, and certainly demonstrates the importance of fins to the species. Just look how huge the pectoral fins are, and the size of that dorsal and tail. It is no wonder that this particular specimen was quite happy holding its position in water as it travelled along at almost five miles an hour.

As a species, the barbel is in every way perfectly designed to feed among the gravels and stones of a bed constantly raked by fast currents.

Any experienced pike angler will probably just have to look at a photograph of the species to be able to form a good impression of where it came from. There are some startling examples. The big news in pike fish-ing today is trout-water pike – pike that grow quick and fat on waters where rainbow trout in particular are stocked. These fish, like the one seen below, are instantly recognizable: they tend to have small heads and be relatively short for their weight. Their shoul-ders are powerful and often a bit humped. Their bod-ies are very broad and frequently very deep. In short, you can be pounds out when trying to guess the weight of one of these fish. I remember once swearing

JUST LISTEN

I suppose I learned to use my own ears on sea trout a good thirty years ago when, by blessed good fortune, I occasionally visited the River Lune during my summer holidays. You could actually hear the water surface fizzing along their scales on a clear night, or at least so it seemed to me then. The sound was electrifying – as exciting as a tug on the line that comes out of the black night.

So how much information can the ears pick up? That splash like a body thrown in in the dark hours of the morning. It was indeed a body, but a fish's, almost certainly either a large carp or, more surprisingly, a pike. Pike often simply leap out on summer nights, perhaps after prey or perhaps simply in search of oxygen, but the roar can easily be heard a quarter of a mile away across water. It is doubtful whether it is worth packing and moving in such cases, however, because the sound can hardly be located with any accuracy.

Much more useful is the ability to distinguish that strange noise known as 'clooping' that only anglers ever hear. Clooping is, of course, the sound a fish makes as it sucks food off the surface of the water – most commonly in the hours of darkness. A loud, short, abrupt noise generally means a carp. If it is longer, with more bubbling and even quite audible sucking sounds, then probably tench or even crucian carp are the culprits. Their mouths are not as big as a carp's and they have to struggle rather more to take in a floating titbit. It is surprising how many times both tench and crucians will take food off the surface at night, especially if it is under a canopy of trees, since this generally intensifies the darkness.

It can also be very useful to be able to distinguish audibly the sound of a rolling fish. A tench breaks surface in the quietest possible way. It is barely audible, and unless the night is absolutely silent you will almost certainly miss it. However, an advantage is that tench will often roll very close to the bank and unless the night is absolutely pitch-black you might momentarily see a dark shadow on the slightly brighter water. A bream rolls more noisily but still with a gentle and controlled movement. There is little splash attached to the action and if you hear one you will probably hear others in the same area for a while before the shoal moves slowly away.

Rudd are the other major rolling stillwater fish and their action is by far the noisiest. A rudd, especially a big one, will often come half clear of the water and land on its side in a joyful prelude to feeding. Where there is one rudd there are generally more and you will probably hear these splashy rolls approaching as they move at quite high speed, looking for food. Very often I have not known that rudd have been present in the water until I have actually heard them and cast a bait in their direction. Then, out of the darkness, comes one of our most beautiful freshwater fish.

Right: I include this shot with a certain amount of reservation, for it is the only water where I have fished at night and been afraid! After years of experience I have become used to all the different sounds of woodland and waterside but here there was a certain menace and chill that I cannot explain and have certainly never experienced elsewhere. This book is all about logic and detection, but what I experienced that night defies both. Perhaps we are wrong to neglect our intuition.

It is half light, and as anglers concentrate on their quivertips, all around them the aquatic world is beginning to awake.

a pike would weigh 17lb and it actually registered 27lb!

Quite different are the pike of Highland lochs, as in the picture below. These are long and lean, with beautiful, torpedo-shaped bodies. The fins appear large for the body size and the fish almost invariably fight like tigers. Another more traditional type of pike is the Broadland fish, seen opposite. This has a distinctive, broad head – when its mouth is open it looks more like a crocodile than a pike. In many cases the body tapers away rather disappointingly, reducing the overall weight of the fish.

Lifestyle variations

All these body shapes reflect lifestyles to a greater or lesser extent: the trout-water pike, for example, probably does not have to work too hard for its food. Stocked rainbow trout have been brought up in stewponds and tend to be ignorant of the menace posed by pike and other predators. They will also group together in large shoals, making hunting comparatively easy. As a result, the pike has a ready source of nutritious, easily caught food, so growth is very rapid.

Nothing could be further from the case in a Highland loch. In all probability, the pike there must spend a great deal of time on the fin, moving through the water looking either for shoals of char or isolated brown trout to pick up. There are long periods when no food at all appears and consequently the pike develops a long, lean, hungry shape. This provides a startling acceleration, for when food does happen by it must not be allowed to escape.

The bucket-heads of Broadland fish have been explained as nature's response to the problem posed by bream shoals. Probably bream, over the centuries, have been the staple diet of many pike in the area and it is just possible that they have developed these broad heads to cope with these deep-sided food fish. Can such structural difference take place over a relatively

TREES

As children most of us learn how useful a tree can be as an observation post. The angler can go on benefiting from trees long after childhood, but the extra body weight leads to obvious dangers. Do use trees for spotting fish activity – in fact, I would say that very often you have to – but never take risks. Be very careful of any branch that looks suspiciously thin, weak or dead, and take great care when climbing in wet weather, when the bark can be very slippery, especially if it has a treacherous coating of moss. Tree climbing is particularly useful in the winter when there are no leaves to block the view and I have done some of my best detection work when there has been a watery winter sun with little wind on the water beneath.

Here I am looking down on a group of very large carp feeding slowly over a clear, hard bottom. The alder provided a perfect vantage point and the fish scarcely, if at all, registered my presence up in the branches above them. However, the trunk was like glass after early-morning rain and the moon boots I was wearing – it was March and still cold – provided minimal grip. Needless to say, I was extra careful, and this should be the rule whenever you climb a tree for fish detection purposes.

short period of time? It appears very possible that this is precisely what happens.

Three photographs of perch are seen opposite, each of which shows how adept perch are at blending in with their environment. Look at the aggressive dorsal fin raised high in the first example – an attitude that the perch always uses when excited, when about to attack or when attacked itself. Note the bold stripes down its back. These are probably an aid to camouflage, both to prevent its being seen by predators and to hide it from small prey fish moving past. It is customary to praise those vivid fins, which are more brilliantly red than you will find on any other fish, even the rudd. This is a fish of around 1lb, growing fast in a clear, rich water.

Water and coloration

Now look at the fish in the second picture. The perch is slightly older and slightly bigger, and its large, hinged mouth is easily appreciated. However, look at its general coloration: you will notice a virtual absence of stripes. This is typical in fish that come from cloudy waters, and is probably explained by the fact that camouflage is not as important to their existence. By and large (and there are always exceptions) such fish will

not grow much above 2lb. Perch hunt largely by sight and in cloudy water their food potential is obviously minimized. In fact, scale readings later showed that this particular perch was near the end of its growth period.

The final example is another interesting case. This perch was caught from a small clay pit where the water has a slight milky tinge. As a result, the perch have adopted the same creaminess in their skin make-up.

Population control

The picture of the roach below tells a story. Clearly it is a big fish, but what are all those clusters of angry red marks? This fish is a survivor of the disease known as columnaris that strikes waters from time to time with devastating efficiency. Often it kills 90 percent of roach in the water but this does mean that the survivors frequently find food is more plentiful and so can grow very fast.

A roach never recovers its original beauty after a columnaris attack and as the wounds gradually heal over the years, they leave pitted scales or gill-flaps and sometimes even entire fins are eaten away. Catch a fish looking like this and there are not likely to be many roach in the water, but what fish there are could be well worth the effort.

A LIVING BAROMETER

Every committed fish watcher and catcher knows that no species likes to feed when the weather has grown suddenly cold or has been stiflingly hot for a long period of time. Clear water also can be disastrous for sport, especially after a leaf fall when there are bright, cloudless skies and frosts begin to set in around late afternoon. Even in summer, a night cold enough to produce widespread dew makes fish reluctant to feed at dawn.

No great skill in detection is needed here, for we are all familiar with those situations in which fishing is bound to be difficult. But what is puzzling is why quite often conditions can seem excellent and yet still the fish do not feed. For example, the weather may have been settled for days and the fish have adopted a quite predictable feeding rhythm. You arrive at the water in high spirits and yet after a few hours go home defeated and puzzled. Soon you see the reason. Quickly, before your very eyes, the weather begins to change radically. If it is winter, mild grey skies begin to be chased away by stark blue ones, and when relatively warm nights are replaced by cruel ones of frost, it kills the fishing stone dead.

Now imagine that it is summer, when a typical situation is that a sun that was benign shortly before is now covered by cold clouds producing a driving rain. The wind might swing in from the north, pick up and soon steam will be rising from the water as it cools by as much as two or three degrees Celsius each hour. As far as feeding is concerned, the fish are just not

A beautiful sight but one that bodes ill for the river fisherman. The night is completely still and the sky contains not a single cloud, indicating that a sharp frost is inevitable. Red sky at night: that band of crimson also indicates that the following day is likely to be crisp and cold and the fishing difficult. Not a night to set the alarm clock!

Look at the frost on the willow branches – and it is eleven o'clock in the morning. However, this is where I decided to fish, close in, in the hope that fish had congregated under the willows for a little encouragement and protection. I was using a stick float, held back severely and fished over depth so that the bait edged through the swim very slowly, allowing reluctant fish every chance to feed.

interested. That much is clear, but how have they picked up the change in the weather so obviously when the frontal system is still in many cases hundreds of miles away? The only plausible answer is that in addition to their highly developed senses of taste, smell and, in some cases, of vision, fish have a powerful ability to sense changes of pressure in the atmosphere.

After five weeks of severe frost on the River Tay, here is a dead salmon that has spawned, begun to return to the sea but died, totally exhausted and washed into a backwater where the ice has formed like great plate-glass windows. Interestingly, roach were beginning to feed that brutal day, probably because they had to. Clearly they must take in some nourishment through the winter and after a while become accustomed to the harshest of conditions.

After a cool night that filled the meadows and valley with mist, this summer morning started very pleasantly. However, the sky is now reddening as clouds approach and the sun begins to blur. A weather front is on its way which may well kill off in the fish all desire to feed.

A day when the fishing looks set to be tough. This is the River Derwent at Chatsworth House in Derbyshire and grayling and chub were the intended targets – both of which feed at very low temperatures. As it turned out, the day was dominated by a succession of rainbow trout, a species that seems hungry whatever the weather. But as the light faded, as commonly happens more coarse fish began to feed, notably dace. No matter how cold the day, it certainly pays to stay at the water until dusk is approaching.

A hybrid if ever I saw one! The head of the fish in the picture above is true rudd, with that protruding bottom lip and golden eye, but thereafter the fish really becomes a muddle. The dorsal fin is set too high up on the body, more in the roach position. And look at the red of the anal and tail fins — splashed on rather than consistent. At a guess, I would say the fish was about 50 percent rudd and 50 percent roach if such a thing is possible. At this size, parentage does not really matter to the angler, but once a fish gets over 2–3lb it really is important to know for sure.

Crucian characteristics

A perfectly proportioned crucian carp is seen in the first photograph opposite — a real golden football of a fish. The shape of the fish does not really qualify it for anything other than life in a stillwater or a very slow-moving river. Just look at the depth of that stomach, which makes it virtually imperative that the fish stands on its head or at least at a steep angle to feed. The short, virtually podgy shape of the fish also explains its unique fighting action when hooked: the runs of a crucian can never be confused with any other species. It is as though the short, fat, muscular body is trying to jag and judder into the bottom of the lake as it seeks sanctuary. There are no long runs — unless you have got a monster. The fish just pulls and tugs and bores down until the pressure becomes too much for it.

The next picture shows a great, olive-green, paddle-finned, red-eyed tench. It is difficult to say what you can learn here. Obviously not a predator's mouth, but from the stockiness of the body and the muscular firmness of the fins, the fish is clearly a very fine fighter indeed. This is a female — in male tench the ventral fins tend to be far bigger and scooped out, shell-like. You can tell, also, that she was caught in mid or late summer, for she carries not an ounce of spawn. The fact that she is long (23in) indicates that if it is heavyweights that you are after then catch her the following June and you are looking at a very big fish indeed.

What else can you tell from this tench? Probably that the water is little fished, for every single thing about her is immaculate. Despite their ruggedness, tench do suffer a great deal from angling pressure: their mouths begin to rip and their fins are very susceptible to keepnet damage. But this is a pristine female, caught probably for the first time in her life.

Two kinds of chub

The chub in the bottom photograph opposite is an interesting one. Most chub seem to fall into one of two categories. The first kind are perfectly scaled and have neat heads, delicate, red-tinged fins and attractive, regularly spaced scaling. The others, like this example, are big-headed, scarred and often with little colour in the body or the fins. I don't think this difference has much to do with fishing pressure or with size or age. Beautiful big chub are taken that have definitely been caught before whereas ugly small fish often appear from nowhere. Nor can a river be said to hold only one or the other type of fish, for often the two live side by side.

This chub is from the River Wye and I don't like the

look of it for other reasons: notice how the head and area around the pectorals tapers away very quickly. This is not uncommon in summer fish that have not really recovered yet from spawning. However, the general leanness indicates to me that it will never really become a big fish and indeed on the Wye any chub of over 4½lb is a rarity.

There is little that can be said really about the dace that is not obvious: it is a slim, silvery fish very much at home in quick, dancing water. Always the big question is the difference between dace and chub and for me the give-away is the mouth. Notice in the shot of the dace opposite how the mouth is small and neat and the lips do not extend back towards the eye, unlike in the bigger, more boldly biting chub. Fittingly, this dace was photographed lying on a water-cabbage leaf, which is probably the most favoured water vegetation of all for the species.

The example shown below is of a fine grayling.

Slender, with small, fine scales, in some ways it is not unlike a dace. And, like the dace, the grayling likes fast-flowing, clean, well-oxygenated water. A fishing detective would know that this fish was caught in the winter: notice how the belly is beginning to fill out as the eggs start to multiply. Many reasons have been put forward for the grayling's great, sail-like size, although sadly, in this photograph the gigantic dorsal fin is not raised to its full height. In all probability, the outsize fin lends greater stability in fast currents but not everybody is happy with that explanation. Why then, they ask, does a trout have such a comparatively small dorsal? Again, why does the grayling have that thin gold pencil line running from the pectoral along the bottom of the stomach? Nobody has come up with an adequate explanation for that either, I'm glad to say. We all need mysteries and if nature were totally explained away it would probably be no more exciting than the internal combustion engine.

USING A BOAT

I do not intend here to explain in detail the use of boats as an angling aid, but simply to stress how great the right sort of craft can be as a tool for the fishing detective. With a suitable boat you can investigate the depths, contours and bottom make-up of any large stillwater. Equally, you can explore a stretch of river very much more fully than it is possible to do from the bank – and this becomes all the more vital the wider the river is.

But best of all, you can see fish at close quarters. Surprisingly, despite what many anglers believe, fish are rarely afraid of a quiet boat. I suppose it is rather like a piece of floating rubbish to them with nothing really very threatening about it. Also, carp in particular seem to see boats as objects of curiosity and will follow them for long distances.

The usual fibreglass or wooden boat is fine but can be rather heavy and unmanoeuvrable. In addition, rowing can be a noisy, splashy activity which will, in fact, disturb some giant species of fish such as rudd. You have also got the problem of loading a boat for transportation by road, and finally you will need at least 6–12in of water before it will float at all – a requirement which rules it out for weedbed investigation.

As a detection aid a canoe is far better. It is easy to transport and light to carry to the bank,

can glide absolutely anywhere and needs only 3–4in of water to float on. The problem with some canoes is that they are slightly unstable and that is where my Kiwi comes into its own. An excellent little craft made by Perception Kayaks, the Kiwi has a very broad beam – 29in against an overall length of 108in – which explains its great stability. In addition, it weighs only some 37lb, so that you can easily put it on a car roof rack or, if necessary, carry it some distance to the waterside.

The Kiwi also has a fine entry bow, a slightly defined keel line and a shallow, arched hole which helps you paddle along a straight line even as a beginner. The large, open cockpit allows you to get in and out easily with little risk of tipping the canoe over. I have been on all kinds of waters in my Kiwi and never felt in the slightest bit of danger, even though I am the cautious type, never take risks and always wear a buoyancy aid.

So small, light and manoeuvrable is this canoe that it hardly creates any disturbance on the water at all. I have had bream actually rub their backs on the underneath of the hull and I have got so close to pike that I have leaned out and dropped a lens on the back of one docile fish, half asleep in the reedbed. You just cannot get closer than that.

Left: This shot was taken in the middle of the summer and shows two fish, both getting on for 30lb, glued together. I had hoped to photograph them in a head-to-tail arrangement, to show how they could easily be mistaken for a monster, but they would never quite pose for me. This behaviour sometimes occurs after normal spawning has taken place, for older fish still seem to feel some residual excitement.

Below: I love this shot for its action and vitality, although the only credit I can claim was for being there in the first place. The carp were so preoccupied that they let me get to within a foot or so of them and the lens was virtually on their backs! In short, spawning carp are completely oblivious of man or any other source of danger and have only one thing on their minds.

CARP DETECTION

THE SPAWNING CARP

For the past half century or so, many writers and anglers have described seeing enormous carp – absolute monsters, in fact. Few, if any, of these observers are liars or fools and they have obviously seen fish quite out of the ordinary. A further examination of many of these sightings shows that they occur in the very early part of the season and, it has been suggested, it is heightened sexual excitement that brings the very largest fish from the depths to show themselves. However, my own observation over many years has led me to believe that this is not so.

Carp exhibit very particular characteristics as they approach spawning: most noticeably, they begin to move in small, tight groups of two or three fish. The important word here is 'tight': they often swim as if they were glued together.

Spawning ritual

It was 18 June 1987 when I saw my own particular monster. A fish the like of which I had never seen before came into view between two islands, swam across the shallows and began to bask only ten yards from me in shallow water. Both its length and breadth were staggering and I realized that I had at last seen a carp of over 50lb. I believed I had seen a carp of over that weight, but it was in fact two mirror carp, both of which I would put in the high twenties, bonded as if they were the same fish as they wheeled around and around in mounting sexual excitement.

Now, both these fish were females. It happened that the lake was an old one and had an ancient strain of carp in it of which about fifteen or twenty remained. All were large and all were female, and although successful spawning obviously did not take place, rituals remained. All carp waters exhibit this type of behaviour as the spawning act approaches. The carp look strangely agitated and move quickly hither and thither, neglecting their traditional patrol routes. Very often one group of fast-moving carp will meet another and there will be a sudden, frenzied explosion of water as they all crash together in a sexual tumult.

This behaviour is determined to a large extent by the weather, but begins as the water begins to move towards optimum spawning temperatures. Sometimes, if a cooling wind chances along, it will go on for days as the carp simply smoulder with pent-up excitement and longing. The longer the 'spawning' is delayed the more dramatic it is when it finally arrives.

An unforgettable spectacle

Carp are often very difficult indeed to tempt during this pre-spawning period. At first you might think otherwise, for, after all, the fish seem to be everywhere, forsaking normal caution and happily exposing themselves and swimming right in front of rods and over lines. And, sadly, right over baited pitches as well!

If the fish are difficult to tempt at this time, then they are quite impossible when the spawning act is upon them. All you can do when they are laying and fertilizing their thousands of eggs is to sit back and gasp with astonishment. Indeed, I have never heard any angler complain at witnessing this spectacle. If the night is

particularly hot and sultry, they will often spawn in the early hours of the morning. But the most common time is sometime after breakfast, when the sun is rising and the morning is really beginning to warm up.

You will probably hear the carp spawning before you see them. There will be brief explosions of water, generally in obscure places behind lily pads or tucked under sunken tree roots. The first groups of fish probably only number four or six or so but as their excitement transmits itself around the lake, the other fast-moving groups of fish home in and join them. Soon you will see twenty, thirty or even forty carp all ploughing together through the silt and the weed, shedding eggs in a crazy piscine orgy.

At this stage the fish are totally oblivious to your presence. You can stand a yard or even less from them and almost bend down and touch the back of a shuddering 20lb mirror. In fact, I have done this and more. I well remember a female leather carp of about 15lb that was hoisted on the water on the backs of attendant males and thrown clean in the air onto the grass bank, where she floundered among the nettles. The

In this typical area chosen by carp for spawning, notice the banks of reeds and the overhanging trees – two types of vegetation against which they love to spawn. They also look for pockets of very still water with currents so weak that their eggs will be in no real jeopardy. The disturbance seen here was made by half a dozen carp, still showing some interest in spawning even though the sun is high and most of the activity has died down.

slope was taking her away from the water's edge and I had to struggle after her, catch her and return her to the swim, where she immediately rejoined the throng.

This is wild, blind, almost violent sex, and as the vast majority of the lake carp population will be involved, fishing during these precious hours is an utter waste of time. Anyway, who would want to interrupt such a vital rite of nature?

Towards noon the explosions may begin to decrease in size and intensity. Little by little, carp begin to move away from the foam-flecked areas to browse on their own, in solitude at last. Within an hour the lake will be quiet again – at least on the surface. But below, everything is wicked activity. Eels, perch and roachlings all gather around the tree and lily roots where the carp were spawning only minutes before. Frantically they slurp in the eggs, and eels in particular will lie against a tree root, gorging themselves until the water is too dark to see into.

Perhaps by late afternoon or certainly early evening, some carp will begin to feed again, and with a vengeance. In all probability, they will not move very far from the places where they spawned and often just slip down into slightly deeper water. Undeniably, in this crucial period their wariness seems often to temporarily desert them: perhaps the adrenaline released by spawning is still carrying them along on a high or perhaps the season is not so far advanced that they are particularly wary anyway. Whatever the truth of the

This picture was taken at two o'clock in the afternoon only yards from where the same fish had been spawning up until eleven-thirty that morning. In fact, the feeding was carried out with exactly the same gusto as the egg laying. I have heard it suggested that the carp are actually returning to feed on their own now fertilized eggs. However, I disagree, for if you watch often enough you will notice that carp return to feed in quite distinct areas, even if only a few yards apart.

matter, certainly excellent catches can be made in a very short time when spawning has just come to an end.

Particle baits

I have generally found that the best bait in this immediate post-spawning period is some form of particle. This is not a hard-and-fast rule, but maggots, casters, hemp and tares and various sorts of nuts have always done very well for me. Perhaps it is because the spawning has churned up the bottom dramatically and released a vast amount of small food items, or perhaps left-over eggs themselves are turning the carp towards very small particles of food. Observation and experience are important, but only intelligent guesses can be made about a great deal of fish behaviour and no matter how skilled the detective there will always be many situations where guesswork is the only recourse.

Understandably, there are those who question the validity of hunting carp so soon after spawning and I think it is certainly only fair to release the fish as soon as they have been caught and not to even consider keeping them in a sack. A quick photograph, preferably right by the water's edge, is all that is needed as a reminder of what can prove one of the most sensational and exhilarating days of the entire carp season.

CARP ON THE SURFACE

One of the great delights of carp is that they are so often visible. Anything like decent weather at all and they will appear, to amuse, entertain and inspire. For me, one of the main attractions is that many of their actions and characteristics you can almost identify with your own. I know all along that they are fish but there is something very engaging about them. So much so, that it is often as satisfying just to watch and try to understand as it is to catch them.

Carp love basking, revelling in pure and simple enjoyment of the sunshine. This is an example of what I mean about human characteristics: they could almost be luscious ladies bronzing themselves on some exotic beach! Look very carefully at binoculars at a basking carp and you will see certain obvious characteristics associated with this relaxed mode. For example, the eye will often roll round in its socket, apparently not fixed on any object at all. Another unmistakable sign is that the pectoral fins remain generally still, often tucked into the body unless they are splayed just to keep balance and position. Any occasional movement of the fish is only incidental.

Right: Often in the summer the water is clear and bright enough for you to see every single detail of the fish you are hoping to catch. If it is carp in particular that you are watching, I defy you not to fall in love with them, for there is something very gentle and serene about the species. This pair are big fish; you can tell that even from a photograph, simply from the bulk of their shoulders and the impressive width of their backs. They are just two of half a dozen inhabitants in a very rich new pit and their growth rate has been exceptional.

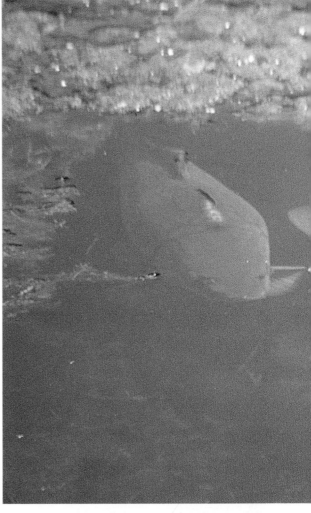

Left: This carp, a great favourite of mine through the summers of 1990–2, could always be seen in this particular hole in the weed, one that it had probably created and kept open for itself. It was a big fish – certainly well over 30lb and probably nearer 40lb, and so its size helped keep me riveted. However, nothing I could do would entice the carp to take bait of any kind and the sessions were full of frustration for me.

One carp habit I really look forward to watching is the occasional lifting and lowering of the dorsal fin. Perhaps the fish simply like exposing this to the sun, almost like you or me stretching or yawning. Sometimes a carp becomes so lazy that it even rolls over to a forty-five-degree angle in the water, exposing its stomach. This does not mean that it is ill in any way, but simply dozing off!

This type of behaviour will often last as long as the sun is high in the sky and the water stays warm. It is not unusual to see the basking position taken up around mid morning in the high summer and last until late afternoon. The carp are simply enjoying themselves with little or no thought of feeding on their mind. Just occasionally a floating bait put near them might attract a response, but generally the splash seems to irritate them and they will drift away into the weed and turn up somewhere else.

The only real success I have had with basking carp is when I have put a large, lively lobworm as close to them as possible without annoying them. Frequently this has to be within a foot or so of their heads otherwise it is most likely to be completely ignored. The problem is that if the worm is taken the fish will still not swim off with it but continue lying where it is, chewing ponderously and thoughtfully before swallowing. Therefore it is really important to watch the line as carefully as possible and if at all feasible, the worm itself, by using binoculars.

You generally see clearly purposeful movement late in the afternoon (or early in the morning) before or after the carp start to bask. Their back ridges repeatedly break through the surface as the fish pursue a very steady course around a familiar patrol route. The tour of the water is very deliberate and everything that seems to offer some potential for food is investigated closely. Often the bow-waves of carp moving in this fashion are extremely visible and can be seen from a hundred yards or more. Because these are fish with food in their mind, it is certainly advisable to up sticks and go after them.

Waters still exist where carp feed in the time-honoured fashion without showing fear of surface baits. Unfortunately, such waters are becoming rarer, which makes it all the more magnificent a sight to see a confident carp approach your bait. The carp will be

Left: Basking carp disturbed in a thick weedbed – a situation typical of fish which, hanging high in the surface water, suddenly become alarmed by the passing of a bird too close, some loud sound near by or, occasionally, being hooked. Once a big fish is startled in this way, it will usually be at least half an hour before it resumes its position.

Below: This photograph was taken at dusk in high summer, which explains its rather sepia-like tones. Each night a very large carp worked exactly the same route, some seventy yards in length, along a reedy bay. You could have set your watch by its comings and goings and it was certainly feeding, to judge from the amount of bubbles that it sent up every now and again along the way. After four days I was confident enough of its routine to put some baits out accurately and not long afterwards I was weighing a fish in the low twenties.

POLARIZING SUNGLASSES

Without good polarizing sunglasses, no fisherman can become a detective, for they are absolutely essential to take the glare off the surface of water. Edwin Land patented his amazing polarizing system in 1929 and founded the Polaroid Corporation in 1937. In doing so he improved dramatically the angler's ability to see beneath the surface. It is not necessary here to go into how polarizing lenses work. But it is important to know that there are great variations in their performance, and therefore it makes sense to buy the most efficient pair you can afford.

Polarizing sunglasses made by Polaroid themselves are widely available from all good chemists and are in the medium price bracket. Good-quality frames are a hallmark of the company and the lenses themselves are of generally fine quality. Optix introduced the polarizing Cormorant range specially for anglers, again at medium price. The lenses themselves come in differing shades but there has been some criticism of their quality, which, it is felt, could lead to eyestrain. However, few would deny the exceptional strength and durability of the frames.

Polarspecs are more expensive but of a

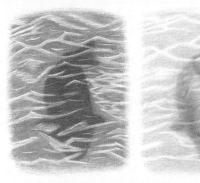

Polarizing sunglasses are probably the most valuable investigation aid the fishing detective can buy. The best examples remove surface glare completely, revealing what is hidden below the surface of reasonably clear water. Their efficiency depends to some extent on the cost, lens colour and the light conditions, but it is nevertheless advisable to carry a pair with you every time you go to the water, even if it is just to observe.

generally high standard and are excellent for adapted use for spectacle wearers. Orvis make very respectable polarizing glasses, some with a small bifocal segment giving 1.7 times magnification – just right for dealing with small knots or helping ageing eyes. Their soft bag is designed to trap air and to float should it fall into the water.

The French company Vuarnet makes Nautilex sunglasses, which offer an alternative to polarizing lenses and are in many situations a better buy. The lenses use internal and reflective filters to drastically reduce glare without impairing vision. Their effectiveness in eliminating dazzle and cutting through haze is remarkable. The wearer can read the surface of the water with great ease, as well as seeing what is happening below. Nautilex sunglasses are towards the upper end of the price range but are an excellent choice for the serious angler.

Your polarizing glasses are an invaluable tool, so look after them and get into the habit of cleaning them regularly. Make sure the frames do not bend otherwise the image is bound to distort, and this is a fault that can not only impair vision through water but also cause headaches. It is a good idea to tie elastic to the earpieces of the glasses so that they will hang round the neck with ease and will not slip off the nose and be lost in a raging torrent.

On their own, polarizing sunglasses are not always quite enough, for light can still seep in unless the rest of the face is shaded. For this reason many matchmen wear green plastic eyeshades, although specialist anglers prefer something a little more subtle! Ian Jones from Wales chooses a large, Australian-type brimmed hat for maximum protection.

Left: Here, in one of my favourite shots of a surface-feeding carp, the fish is approaching loose feed with absolutely no trepidation. Its eyes are fixed firmly on the bait and not looking for line, controller floats or anything else. The carp certainly liked the taste of the food and soon afterwards began to ride ever higher in the water, with its back well out and its eye and gill flaps often showing. This is the most confident feeding mode you will ever find, and in these circumstances it is unlikely that a carp will show much suspicion of your bait.

Right: This handsome 10lb mirror carp was on the point of taking a small biscuit when it saw my camera lens and bolted in terror. Nor did I see it again that day after this scare.

moving very slowly and very positively, for it has nothing to fear and its movements reflect its peace of mind. As it approaches food, the fish will lift its head well clear of the surface. By this I mean that the water-line will in many cases be beneath the fish's eye. It will approach food very calmly, quite decisively and the takes will be slow and deliberate. The food will disappear between the lips with absolutely no hesitation from the fish. A confident carp will eat three to eight pieces of food, depending on its size, before dropping from the surface and turning away to chew and swallow. As soon as this process is completed, the confident, hungry carp will be back on the surface searching again. A big piece of bait – the traditional matchbox -sized crust – will be attacked noisily as the fish gulps and slobbers in an attempt to fit the piece between its lips. Fish like these are almost shamefully easy to hook, but they very soon acquire their own wisdom – make no mistake about that.

As I said earlier, it is rare to find carp showing all the signs of relaxation on the top! The angling detective will very quickly be able to see which carp are in fact nervous when it come to taking baits on the surface. Typically, a sophisticated fish will make a very fast approach into a group of baits and pick off one or two pieces, often noisily, before departing, generally for good. The fish's whole approach is tense and edgy and

Below: Some carp approach baits in a positive manner, with their backs out of the water as they feed. You will notice that a confident carp moves far more slowly than a scared one, as though it has all the time in the world.

you can sense its relief as it moves away to chew the pieces it has sneaked.

A sophisticated carp will approach even free baits – never mind those on a hook – with extreme caution and often 'boil' repeatedly underneath them. What happens – and you can see this clearly through binoculars – is that the fish comes to within 2–3in of the surface, opens its mouth and then dives down again in

suspicion. If that distrust turns to fear – let us say the carp has seen a line or a controller float – then the boil will in actual fact become an explosion of water. The fish now really panics and slaps the water with its tail as it plunges out of the danger zone.

Another hallmark of the sophisticated fish is to come very close to baits, watch them for half a minute, nose them or even stroke them with the tail and then

I began to wonder why the carp seemed invariably to browse on the top in one part of a particular lake and yet would go down to feed off the bottom elsewhere in the same water. After wading for a while I found the answer: the lower water is cooled by springs entering the lake, whereas the upper water is warmed by the sun. I measured the temperature of both areas and found that there was a dramatic difference of 6°C (11°F) between them. Comparing data in this way often illuminates what might otherwise remain a mystery.

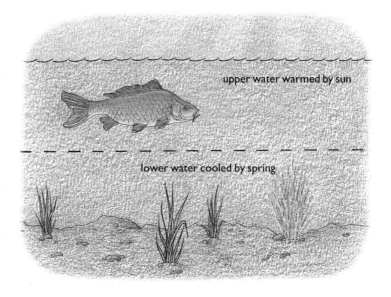

upper water warmed by sun

lower water cooled by spring

move on without ever having opened its mouth at all. Bigger baits, such as bread or cake baked for the purpose, will often be broken up either with the tail or the body and then small, sinking pieces taken at leisure. Alternatively, the fish simply appears out of nowhere, takes one single bait and is never seen again. In fact, this appears to be quite common, as though even the most sophisticated fish cannot resist just one bite but

Below: From the point of view of detection, there is a significant link between carp and wind. When a strong wind blows up they seem to be pushed around the water in front of it, and at other times they behave as if they are aware of wind strength and direction, apparently knowing that it will bring them food on the surface. When fishing surface baits it pays to place them on the wind channels so that they will be carried to the fish in the most natural way.

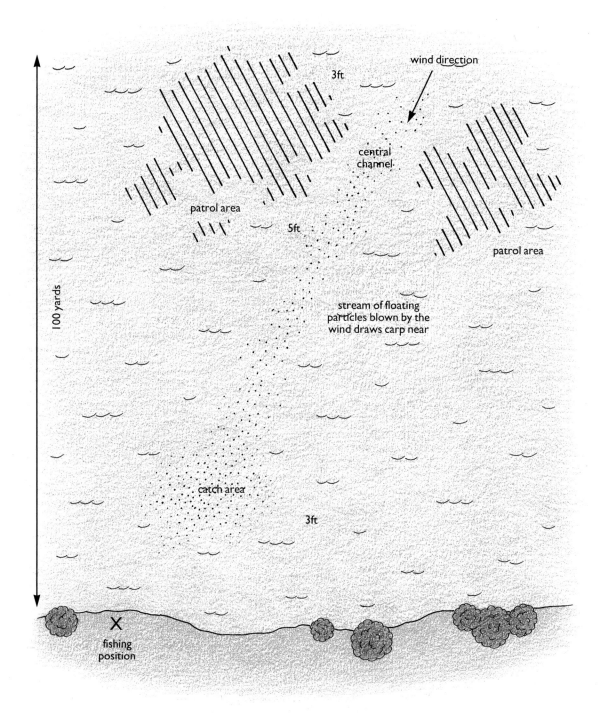

A large leather carp in the bay of an old estate lake that appears to hold few fish although all of them grow to a good size. Curiously, these fish are rarely seen taking food from the surface even though the water is shallow and warms up nicely and would seem to be a perfect surface-bait water. But it certainly is not for want of trying, for at times I have plastered the surface with the most tantalizing of floating baits. It is one of those mysteries I have yet to unravel, but I know that detective work will play a major role here.

knows it is pushing its luck to come back for more.

Surface fishing for carp began in the 1960s and during the 1980s developed real momentum. Over the years a wide variety of gimmicks have been invented to fool the sophisticated carp into taking the bait. Most of these last only a very short time before the carp wises up. The successful surface-carp angler uses lines as light as he can safely get away with, and often the last couple of yards will be of the new, ultra-thin copolymer material. Remember too that a sunken line is less obvious than a floating one, and that choppy water tends to mask the line better than a very still surface. If you can lay line over thick weed or a lily pad so much the better. Sometimes you will find a carp feeding in the thick scum which has built up at the end of a hot day and this can also mask line to a great degree.

It is important to present free-floating baits effec-tively. Never scatter them all over the lake otherwise the carp will simply become dispersed and no real feeding pattern will emerge. The more you watch carp or any other fish, the more you will realize that they will click into a feeding mode, and this applies to even the most wary of them. Therefore, if you keep feeding baits steadily down a wind lane you will tend to attract carp to it and they will begin to pick off food. Do not be in too much of a hurry to cast out a bait, but let them build up confidence. Then again, avoid putting too many baits out or you will take the edge off the carps' hunger. This is where detection comes in: you must really watch what the carp are doing and think about every action they make; on most waters, simply heaving out a lot of baits and fishing haphazardly will bring no result at all.

Do not mistake oblivious fish for sophisticated fish. There are some waters, even quite heavily fished waters, where the fish rarely, if ever, take a floating bait even though they are quite happy to appear on the surface. They can swim past baits all summer and simply not realize they are food. You can tell they are oblivious rather than sophisticated because you will sometimes see them emerge with a bait on their back! Many theories have been put forward about oblivious fish but nobody has really come up with a full answer – another mystery for the detective to solve!

BINOCULARS

A good pair of binoculars is an invaluable piece of equipment that every fishing detective should consider investing in. Not only do they allow you to spot and observe far-off fish activity, but you can also keep an eye on a floating bait presented some distance out, so that you can increase your range.

Binoculars are classified by the two figures on the body of the instrument. The first number is the multiplication factor, for example 7, 10 or 12. In the latter case, for example, 120 yards is brought down to 10 yards. The second figure is the diameter of the lens in millimetres – generally 40 or 50. This is vital to the amount of light that is allowed into the image that you see. The rule is to divide the magnification into the lens diameter to obtain the light factor. So, for example, a pair of my binoculars are rated 12 x 40. These magnify greatly but their light allowance is only around 3.3, making them poor for fish observation in obvious light. My other binoculars are set up at 7 x 50. Their magnification is less dramatic but, with a light factor of 7.1, they are perfect for dawn, dusk or winter work. On balance, I find the 7 x 50s the most useful and as well as being easier to focus they are far less prone to shake in anything stronger than a breeze.

The other major consideration is glass quality. As usual, you get what you pay for and it is important to take the binoculars out of the shop and test them very thoroughly in the street. Compare rigorously the performance of all the models that you are considering and, if possible, return to the shop in different light levels to make sure the pair that you finally pick will cope with everything that you might demand of them.

Binoculars are ideal as a fish-spotting aid, even for watching floats at long range or pieces of floating food offered to carp. They can also enrich the day by being used to observe bankside wildlife such as these birds, whose nesting activities were first studied with binoculars.

feather   leaf

By using binoculars the angler can see in detail what is happening both in his swim and in the water as a whole. However, a common problem is overestimating the size of fish as a result of the lenses' magnification. It is a good idea to take account of the true size of a natural object, such as a feather or leaf, which is located near to the fish, so that a sense of the fish's size can be gained when both are seen through the binoculars.

Every so often an oblivious fish actually takes a bait into its mouth. The trouble is, once the fish has taken the bait it simply lies with it in its mouth, neither chewing nor swallowing. This is another occasion where binoculars come in useful, for you can watch the bait and strike the instant it disappears. Believe me, that will be one utterly surprised carp.

Imagine the scene: the sun is beginning to set behind the trees and it is around nine o'clock on a warm, high-summer evening. What wind there was has died hours ago and now the lake is absolutely flat calm. There are still swallows and martins over the water but the first of the bats is appearing and a couple of herons are flying in for their evening's hunting.

Of particular interest is the surface of the lake. If you look very carefully you will notice that it is completely ringed with rising midges, as if a light rain were falling. The conditions are ideal for a massive hatch of midges and countless millions are disappearing up into the air. Look even more carefully at where the water is still

Carp often spend the daylight hours in dense weed, seemingly uncatchable. However, they are likely to prove susceptible to a worm, provided it remains on the surface and cannot burrow out of sight. The trick is to snip the ends off so that it loses orientation. A small piece of cork or polystyrene on the hook should stop it sinking and becoming masked by weed. A float is important here to give an indication of the take, which is often very gentle.

and covered with the scum of the day. In the falling light, you might just see the water hump and move, welling steadily. Get closer, moving very slowly and quietly, and you will see the backs of carp just cleaving the surface in a slow, positive fashion. Quite often you will see the head of the fish, the eye, and even the top of the mouth as it skims the surface film before the fish disappears, leaving behind it a small trail of bubbles.

What is happening is quite simple: exactly like trout taking buzzers on a reservoir, the carp are sucking in the struggling midges as they throw off their shucks and escape into the air as fully formed insects. Scoop out a little of the filmy water and you will find that it is alive with wriggling insects. Probably each fish takes hundreds of tiny food items into its mouth on each of its excursions to the surface. It is fascinating that carp of well over 20lb will feed in this way, happy to dine delicately on such tiny organisms.

Scaling down

To catch one of these fish is a triumph in itself and the ideal approach would be to use fly tackle and tie on a small red buzzer to a tapering leader. But then few of us carry fly-fishing gear along with our normal carp tackle, and I have had most success by attaching a matchstick-sized float 5–6in above a hook of size 14 or thereabouts, baited with a small brandling, half a redworm or a maggot-and-caster cocktail. The hook needs to be small because the carp are really pre-

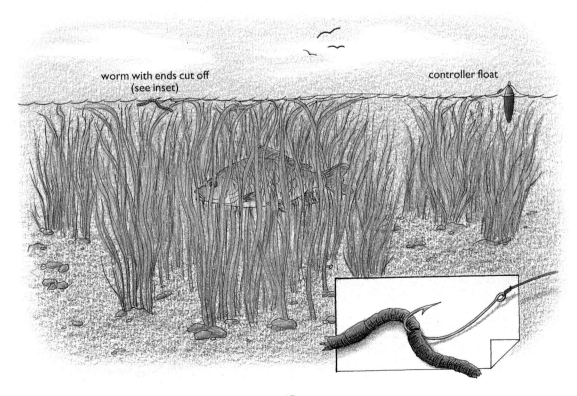

worm with ends cut off
(see inset)

controller float

occupied with tiny items and will shy away from anything large or clumsy. The line should also be as delicate as snags and weed allow. This is an ideal situation for the new generation of Japanese copolymer lines, as these offer such a superb strength-to-diameter ratio. A hooklength of 8lb b.s. should be ideal, and will only be as thick as conventional 5lb line.

Simply cast the bait into the patch of a nymphing carp and perhaps twitch it a little as the fish approaches. Nine times out of ten the offering is ignored but you are likely to see enough carp and have enough opportunities to land one or two before complete darkness sets in.

Of course, the waterside needs to be very quiet for this type of fishing and it is often likely that the most hectic nymphing activity will take place in the shallow, snaggy overlooked backwaters of any lake. Fishing is all about satisfaction, and this is certainly a lovely way to take these fascinating fish. Above all, it can be quite a practical one: the fish are not used to being pursued in this manner and very often they will prove suckers for a method they have never seen before.

A final thought. The sun is down and the shadows

This is one of the most extraordinary photographs I have ever taken and one that reveals a huge amount about the feeding habits of carp. Look at the picture closely and you will see little 'holes' in the top central part. Beneath these are carps' mouths and the water and the insects in it are being sucked down, causing this vortex effect. On this occasion, this type of feeding went on for some forty-five minutes and at least ten carp were involved. I am in no doubt that the food they were taking was midges struggling on the surface to be free of their cases. Likewise, small moths and other insects were sucked in if the fish came across them. In the light of this shot, it is all the more strange that most carp anglers do not think of their quarry as committed insect eaters.

have joined together. The moon is not far from rising and all is dark and quiet – apart from occasional slurps from the scum in front of you, where the carp are now feeding on the flotsam of the day. Find a live moth or, better still, have a few artificials tied up ready somewhere in your tackle. Cast these out under the same small float and draw them back very slowly in a twitchy way across the surface film. What a way to take a fish at the end of a splendid evening.

CARP ON THE BOTTOM

Around about five o'clock in the afternoon on most summer and early-autumn days the sun will begin to lose a little of its power and perhaps even drop behind the trees. Shadows lengthen over the water and the heat is obviously less intense. Things begin to change in a very subtle way and the carps' movements begin perceptibly to speed up. You will see them move around the weedbeds, often a foot or more away from them. The dorsal fin will be raised more frequently and the tail fin will begin to do its first real work of the day. Eventually a carp or two will begin to leave the weeds or the placid water and drift slowly away into open water. Slowly, more and more carp will follow and you can be sure that the serious task of the evening and night is about to begin.

Feeding signals

At first you will see the fish on the surface cruising slowly but then, slowly and gradually, they will begin to leave the surface and eventually drop totally out of sight. This is the sign that you have been waiting for: the carp are almost certainly going down to feed and it could well be that in a short time you will see bubbling

A number of large carp are leaving the shallows and gradually dropping down the lake as the sun sinks and the water cools. Feeding is very much on their minds.

or even smoke-screening. Let us look at both these tell-tale signs.

One of the greatest excitements a carp angler can experience is to see a fish come into his swim, stop, sink a little in the water, tip its head down and disappear from view. With any luck at all, a few seconds later the first bubbles will begin to rise to the surface – a sure sign of a feeding carp. Bubbles have long been recognized as spelling carp, and no carper can see them without an increase in pulse rate! But how does the fish make bubbles?

An old theory is that as it buries its head into that layer of animal, vegetable and mineral deposits over the bottom of the lake the carp disturbs oxygen, which rises in bubbles. After many, many hours of watching carp feed, I don't think this explanation is sound. Test it for yourself. Take a rod rest, shove it into the bottom silt and see what type of bubbles rise to the surface. Sometimes bubbles do appear, but they tend to be large, single and smelly, very unlike the stream of tiny ones that a feeding carp produces.

My own theory is that as the carp pushes its head into the layer of silt its barbules probe around feeling for bloodworm, nymphs and any other living organisms. Once the carp has located wriggling lifeforms it begin to suck, and in sucking it takes in food, oxygen and bottom debris. The oxygen – or at least some of

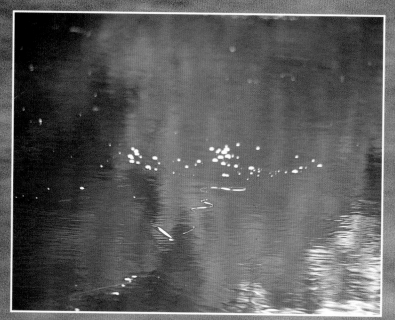

Left: A carp is hard at work, sending up legions of bubbles. In these cases, when the distance is not too great I definitely prefer to use a float rather than leger tackle. The reason is that if the carp does not take the bait straight off, it is a very easy matter to reel in and recast where you see it go down again. The whole thing takes a matter of seconds and involves very little disturbance compared with legering.

Main picture: Two carp feeding very slowly in the late morning. In this water most feeding activity takes place around dawn and early morning and by this time is slowing down appreciably. Notice how the carp are heading for the sandy area, a typical stopping-off point.

Right: The carp can be seen feeding quite clearly in just under 3ft of water, pushing up an area of mud as it advances. Also visible are small strings of bubbles issuing from its gill flaps, and this one of the few photographs that I know of that shows this particular bubbling action at such close range.

Above: This shot captures one of those occasional times when a group of carp really gets its head down and feeds completely without caution. The bait was a mass particle concoction of hemp and tares which the fish found absolutely irresistible.

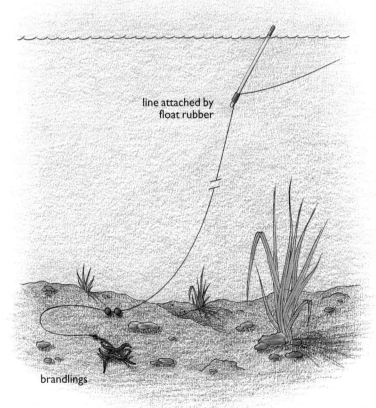

line attached by
float rubber

brandlings

Left: In this perfect, if old-fashioned, set-up for bubbling carp the float is simply an old quill, attached at the bottom end only, so that the line sinks to some extent and the wind's influence is avoided. Brandlings are as good a bait as any, simply because they are the sort of food bubblers are looking for.

it – filters out through the gill-flaps in the form of bubbles. More oxygen, the food and some of the rubbish also passes down the throat into the stomach and again bubbles are produced – this time leaving the vent. As a result, it is not unusual to see two distinct trails of bubbles leaving a feeding carp.

I believe that to some extent the amount of bubbles created depends on how heavily the fish is feeding. For example, I have seen many carp browsing half-heartedly and just producing the odd patch of bubbles here and there. This sight is very common in cold winter waters when all activity is rather lethargic. On the other hand, I have seen two of three carp enter an area, dive and really plough into the bottom as though their lives depended upon it. At these times bubbles rise with such ferocity that they actually fizz on the surface and you can watch the trail left by the carp as they meander around below.

Tiny food items

One thing I am sure of is that carp tend to make more bubbles when feeding on small foodstuffs than they do when they are taking in large items. After all, in the wild, carp are probably used to feeding on tiny foodstuffs – the largest bloodworm is rarely more than half an inch long and weighs a fraction of an ounce and many aquatic animals are much smaller than this. Bubbles therefore come naturally as the carp feeds, as they do when it browses over maggots, casters, hempseed, corn even, and other particles. However, if a carp is simply wandering along, tipping up to take the odd large boiled bait then you do not see nearly as many, if any, bubbles.

Nor am I completely happy with the idea that carp always, or even usually, feed amid the bottom layer of decaying remains. On the contrary, it is extremely common to see carp pass over weeded, dirty areas of a lake in search of clean, polished patches of the bed made up of gravel and sand. It is interesting to study the bubbles that they produce over these tabletop-sized areas. The bubbles are rarely of the fizzy, frothy kind and mostly come up in small, almost self-contained groups. Possibly the carp are feeding less energetically, but I am not sure that this is always the case.

Float tactics

Catching carp obviously takes precedence over simply indulging in speculation, but the fact remains that bubbling carp are very catchable provided you read the bubbles correctly and fish the right way. If they are feeding on natural foods – that is not over your own bait – then you stand very little chance of catching them on large, artificial foodstuffs. Far better to try maggots, casters or small red worms – the smaller the

A good-sized mirror carp forages in silt overlying a hard bottom. It is not clear exactly where the bubbles come from, but they may well escape through the gills to explode on the surface. Another possibility is that some bubbles rise up as intestinal gas is expelled. Whatever the explanation, never underestimate the value of bubbles as a clue to activity, and learn to recognize the difference between them and the release of gas from the bed of the water.

better, and perhaps bunched on a size 16 hook. Naturally, whatever bait you use should be presented on the bottom and sometimes a shot can even pull it into the layer of sediment, where, if it is felt, it will be taken. However, I do prefer the bait to be visible to the fish – for obvious reasons. My own preference is to present the bait under a float, and I have had a good deal of success with baits suspended above the bottom by no more than half an inch or so. It is likely that a carp will take such a bait either as it goes down or comes up before or after feeding.

Bubbling carp are generally not as easily scared as you might think. They appear to have feeding very much on their mind and generally their eyes are directed very much downwards. This can give you a chance to get in close and present your bait exactly where you want it and even to manoeuvre it into the path of a feeding fish. This is where a float again scores over the more conventional leger. Try pulling a bomb-fished bait along the bottom to place in front of a moving fish

Left: A carp heading for a cleared patch on a lake bed. The question arises of whether the patch already existed or the carp has made it by feeding there. In the absence of a definite answer, suffice it to say that once they have selected a place carp will continue to feed there and keep any algal growth away. Sometimes I think that such areas are chosen because one or more springs enter the lake there.

Right above: In this perfect illustration of smoke-screening, several fish are ploughing into the bottom, strongly colouring the water.

Right below: Two fish break away from the main group and move off fast, occasionally stopping to smoke-screen again. Other fish are also disappearing, or moving quickly and halting every now and again to burrow into the silt.

and all you will do is pick up great piles of dead leaves and branches. On the other hand, a float, by giving you far greater versatility, allows you to get the best out of bubbler fishing.

I believe it was Richard Walker, in his classic *Stillwater Angling*, who coined the phrase 'smoke-screening'. According to Walker, the term 'describes a fish that works along the bottom and leaves a long trail of disturbed mud. This is not the same as bubbling; it can be done without raising any bubbles at all. Sometimes just a few fine bubbles come up. Smoke-screening fish will often take a bait carefully in their path.'

Feeding over silt

Smoke-screening fish are almost always feeding fish but – and this is the interesting point – bubbles, as Walker said, are not associated with this particular action. So it is reasonable to assume that the carp are feeding in some different manner. Indeed it seems to me, after many hours of detection, that smoke-

screeners are moving rather more quickly than bubblers and possibly sucking up food from above the bottom silt rather than from beneath it. I suspect that this is a crucial difference and it suggests that the carp are feeding on different foodstuffs altogether. In fact, it is quite usual to see carp smoke-screening over baits that are lying on the bottom: presumably they do not need to dig for these and so there are no bubbles.

A smoke-screener is probably easier to catch than a bubbler and has an eye open for larger foodstuffs than the minute organisms of most lake beds. This means that there is more chance of your larger, obvious artificial bait being taken. It is a useful thing to remember that the thicker the mud stirred up, the less likely your terminal tackle is to be seen. I have often noticed this in action: in shallow, clear waters carp can be very suspicious of leads, lines and floats, but once they have really stirred the bottom into a soup they are far more likely to be unaware of the tackle and caught that much more easily.

USING THE SUN

Good light is absolutely essential if the angler wants to investigate sub-surface. A strong sun and clear water really do open up the world of the fish in a most amazing fashion. By and large the sun is at its best from around ten o'clock in the summer or a little later in the winter and fish spotting can remain excellent until the sun dips sometime in the early to late afternoon. Ideally, for best viewing, the sun should be behind the angler. The trouble is this can also cast a shadow so great care has to be taken. If the sun is in front of you there is no problem with the shadow but the surface glare is much increased and often impenetrable. It really does pay to consider the sun's angle when you are making a detection attack on any water.

Mind you, light is a funny thing. I have known certain lakes respond best visually on dull days when the sun actually has been hidden by cloud. You do not see great detail in such weather but it is often quite possible to see the shapes of fish comparatively distinctly and deduce their patrol routes and feeding stop-offs. Naturally, the real killer is a wind strong enough to put a chop on the surface: it is a nightmare trying to see through a ripple, especially if light is variable.

I am rather attached to this photograph, as it took a great deal of work to obtain. A large mirror carp moves off a clear, sandy bottom after having spent a short time feeding there during the early winter of 1992. The water is about 3ft deep, but the light, although dim, seemed perfect for photographing this dark fish and drab surroundings. I cannot quite say why but brighter sunlight did not improve things at all. Indeed there was something about the overcast weather that helped photography, and the fishing, to a great degree. I later caught the fish, which weighed just over 18lb.

The sunnier the day the more likely the fishing detective is to have a good view of what is going on in the water. Although you should aim to have the sun behind you, it can cast your shadow on the water if you adopt a position like the angler in the first illustration. If you expect to see fish unobserved, do not stand on an open section of bank, but instead use every possible source of cover – a tree, for example, as in the second drawing, or tall vegetation – so that you cast no shadow or, if you do, it is broken up.

CARP IN SANCTUARY

An important feature of carp behaviour is that, in heavily and lightly fished waters alike, they take advantage of areas that offer sanctuary. It is tempting to think that such areas are only associated with environments that see a lot of anglers and a lot of pressure, but this is not so. There is something in the carp's mentality that will very often lead it to look for a safe haven even when anglers are almost unknown at that water. I can think of many private waters where access is almost totally denied but where carp still enjoy the safety and security of their own particular sanctuary. It is just a characteristic of the carp's mental make-up, but not incomprehensible. After all, we enjoy the peace our own homes bring us.

'Invisible fish'

It is very important to remember that a carp can make itself almost invisible and that sanctuaries therefore can be difficult to pinpoint. For example, think of the well-documented monsters of Redmire Pool. Many reputable anglers over many years have sworn that they have seen enormous fish in this very small lake. Nothing remarkable in that apart from the fact that the fish will then go missing for months or even years and are sometimes only spotted perhaps two or three times in a decade. How on earth can this happen? My own experience of 'invisible' fish is also a strong one: a three-acre lake near my home held a large leather carp who was well known to all the anglers that fish there. What only a handful of people realized was that the water held a common carp at least as big (if not a fair bit bigger) than this very friendly, easily seen leather. I myself only saw the common on one occasion even though I fished the water regularly over many years and for two seasons absolutely haunted the place. The point is that when they want to, carp can make themselves very difficult to see and often you must seek out their sanctuaries.

The most obvious sanctuaries are overgrown bays – those little inlets in the bank where trees have fallen in and a network of branches criss-cross the water. If these bays are along an inaccessible or remote part of the bank, the carp are all the more likely to head there.

Islands have always been attractive to carp, especially those looking for a little bit of peace. It is re-

There is a 25lb mirror carp in this photograph, which was taken just 4ft from the fish. The water is only shallow and yet the fish is virtually totally hidden by the water iris; it was only the vibration of the plant that led me to see it at all. A float set-up with a worm fished hard into the roots of the iris nearly succeeded, but I missed the bite.

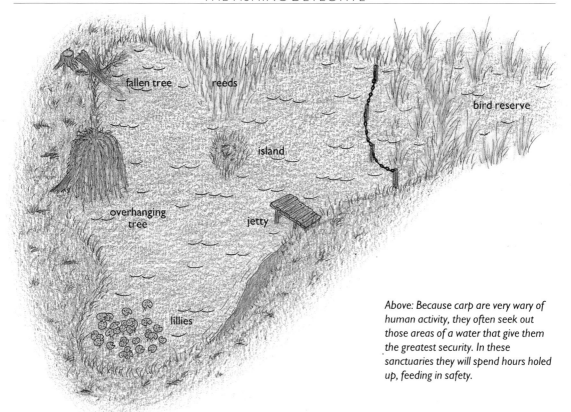

fallen tree

reeds

bird reserve

island

overhanging
tree

jetty

lillies

Above: Because carp are very wary of human activity, they often seek out those areas of a water that give them the greatest security. In these sanctuaries they will spend hours holed up, feeding in safety.

Left: In the caption on page 37 I wrote about the big carp that stayed put in its hole in the weeds and nearly drove me to distraction. Eventually I decided to get in the water and, with a friend's help, set about removing the weed altogether. It seemed like a good idea at the time, but it was a disaster. The carp simply left for another part of the water and I saw no sign of it again all that summer! You have to do something in a frustrating situation like that, and even if nothing else is achieved you learn by your mistakes.

Right: Carp in sanctuary are often very nervous, so it pays to take great care to conceal your presence. It is a good idea to drape the netting that duck shooters use along a fishing platform and cover it with various bits of plant and vegetation. Carp will swim very close to such a pitch, fearing nothing at all.

CARP AT REST

In summer it can be an instructive experience to don shorts or swimming trunks and wade out into a carp water – provided, of course, that it is allowed and you are not annoying other anglers. You will often find that after a day of sunshine the top layers of water are very warm, whereas your feet and ankles and shins are quite cold. I have frequently recorded a difference of several degrees Celsius between the surface and the bottom of a 4ft swim. Presumably what happens is that the sun warms the top layers much faster than the bottom water, which can be kept cool by incoming springs. My hydrology is at best rudimentary, but at least this appears to be common sense and it may well explain why resting carp almost invariably choose to lie close to the surface.

Like most of us, carp are lovers of the sun and you see them most at ease on bright, warm days in high summer, from about ten o'clock onwards. Again like humans, I believe that they like company. Often groups of fish bask together in one small piece of water that seems no different from any other, and in such instances I can only assume that they have formed some little club-like bond.

When in a sociable mood, carp always seem to choose placid water, where the wind is kept off, where scum has built up and the water has a nice, rich, oily sheen. Failing that, very often they will be found among weed. Clearly carp and weed are obviously in complete harmony, especially during the heat of the day when the weed itself probably gives off a little warmth and certainly affords security. Carp seem to love weed of all sorts and their affection for lily pads is legendary. In fact, some long-established lily beds have become like citadels for the entire carp population of a particular water and the wary fish will not leave the bed throughout the hours of daylight.

Carp at rest can virtually merge with their surroundings and it pays to walk around a water extremely slowly, scrutinizing every square yard of water. This particular fish had drifted to rest by a large mat of weed and took quite some seeing.

Above: I alarmed this small group of carp in a medium-sized pit by trying to get too close to take photographs. They took fright, but I was able to follow them a hundred yards into a small bay covered with floating duckweed, where they hid for over an hour.

Below: Carp give out many clues in the form of body language, notably when they are frightened. Many things can alarm a carp, in particular bait or end tackle that it associates with a bad experience. However, the first sign you are likely to spot is a cloud of silt, and perhaps the carp's back, as the fish flees to its safe haven.

markable how close to the bank of an island a carp will hang, pressed right in under the trees, even sometimes under the roots themselves. Indeed, when in sanctuary, the carp will not move more than a foot or two from the island and the further the island is from the public bank the better the carp will like it.

Thick, established lily beds are well-known carp sanctuaries in which the fish feels pretty well invincible and often will only move out after darkness. In addition, any quiet backwater in a lake will serve as a sanctuary and so what we must look for is somewhere that

WADERS

Thigh waders, or even better chest waders, are excellent aids for the fishing detective. It is amazing how close fish will come to an angler standing quietly in the water. At times I have had tench feeding within a yard of me and barbel actually rubbing themselves on my waders! This is entertaining, but with patience you should be able to benefit from the situation, for you can learn a great deal about fish behaviour from such close quarters.

If the weather and water are warm enough you can simply wade in, bare-legged and with perhaps an old pair of trainers or plimsolls to protect your feet. The water will need to be warm, however, if you are to bear it for more than a few minutes at a time. And be careful of little waterfleas, which can inflict troublesome bites on naked flesh.

In Britain the water is not always warm enough for prolonged immersion, and this picture of me photographing barbel was actually taken in the south of France in the middle of a heatwave! What surprised me during this and other expeditions used to build up a useful photographic record of barbel was just how close to my legs they would come. It was not unusual to have them feeding within 2–3ft of my plimsolls. Other anglers have also remarked on this, and when some of them have been fishing in midwater they have noticed barbel actually beneath their legs picking up pieces of fallen bait. Such observations serve to confirm that fish are usually much more wary of anything on the bank than in or on the water, where they seem to show far more tolerance.

offers peace, protection and security from the prying eyes of the angler – the one predator the carp really fears once it has grown bigger than a couple of pounds. Make no mistake: carp recognize us as a foe.

There is, I admit, something a little underhand about fishing for carp in their sanctuaries. The last thing we want to do is to inflict real mental scars on fish that we love and if we pursue them too much in these supposedly inviolate places there is a chance of making them very neurotic. In fact, this has happened in some well-documented cases. Carp need places to get away, again rather like us. If we must hunt carp in this way, it is only fair to fish for them with tackle substantial enough to land them if hooked. Remember that a sanctuary is chosen because it offers security and there are bound to be snags, often vicious ones, in close proximity to the fish. Bear all this in mind when choos-

ing rods, lines and hooks, and weigh up the risks.

Often, sanctuaries can be discovered by watching out for scared fish. A carp will be positively alarmed if it is hooked and lost and sometimes if you follow the bow-wave or the fish itself it will lead you to a safe area where it will sulk for anything from a few hours to several days. Not that a carp needs to be physically hurt to become frightened. It could be that just the sight of a line or a feared bait will send it fleeing to its haven. A frightened fish is easy to pick out: it will swim very quickly, the tail fin really working hard from side to side, propelling it through the water like a torpedo. Very often silt, debris and streams of bubbles will be thrown up as the carp flees to its own private place. There is absolutely no point in trying to fish for it once it has taken flight. A frightened carp is most unlikely to feed for many hours, so simply let it be.

WINTER CARP

Carp-watching in winter is very much better than you would think, provided you can stand the cold. The water is often at its very clearest after the first frosts have killed off any daphnia or algae that cloud the water in summer. This can mean that from November onwards carp lakes are strikingly clear, so that every single scale and fin ray of a carp can be observed.

Also, as the water begins to drop in temperature, carp are more and more likely to take up semi-permanent residence close to banks and especially under trees. I am not quite sure why they do so, but perhaps the soil radiates some heat into the water, or the overhead branches form a canopy of shade and protection from the winds, or maybe both factors apply. In any case, now that the leaves have gone from the branches and cannot obscure your view, it is a good time to climb trees and observe what the carp are doing.

Cold-weather feeding

You would expect the carp to have slowed down quite considerably. Indeed almost always their movements become very slow and ponderous. It is very exciting to watch big fish, especially at this time of year: somehow their lethargy adds grace and majesty to the way they hover and drift in the clear water. Now they really are like great dark-purple airships hovering over

the lake bed. In my experience, only on very few occasions have carp appeared totally comatose. In fact, I have often watched them moving under the ice, obviously awake, alert and even feeding. I have even caught carp as ice was forming around my line where it entered the water, so do not be put off by the coldest of temperatures.

Nevertheless, temperature is important and the lower it falls the less active the carp are. But I believe that light is at least as crucial a factor. I know that you would expect cold, clear days to be virtually useless and that the carp would hate such weather, but this is far from being the case. In fact, I have often found these high-pressure times very productive. After the night frost the fish can be very docile at dawn and in the early morning, but as the sun rises things begin to change. Around midday and on into the afternoon carp will certainly show signs of interest and probably begin

Two big carp glide in from the middle of the lake to a bankside swim, looking ghostly in the clear water. It is in the early afternoon, a time when feeding activity is particularly high on this lake. My float is just visible above the tip of the tail of the second fish. However, it was not long before they began to be afraid of both the float and the line falling from it through the water and I had to switch to legering.

Above: On the same lake as in the picture on page 61, a good-sized fish drops from the surface and begins to move down over some baits.

Below: The sight all carp anglers love to see: the flash of a mirror's belly as it turns and drops vertically to the lake bed. It can only be doing one thing: feeding. Shortly afterwards the line twitched and I was playing a very good carp.

JUDGING THE WEIGHT OF FISH

Watching fish in the water is absolutely fine but it is very easy to misread the evidence. Water plays the strangest tricks of all and the size of fish can be very deceptive. The old story told to me by my grandmother was that water magnifies and that in actual fact a fish looked bigger in the water than it actually was on the land. This, with all respect to the dearly loved old lady, is often nonsense. In fact, in very clear water a fish always looks a lot smaller than it is and this impression is increased greatly the deeper the fish is swimming.

I remember well fishing for tench in one deep, very clear lake where my partner and I guessed that most of the fish weighed 4–5lb. The first fish weighed 6lb 2oz and as it slid back we realized that it was certainly one of the smaller ones and that most of the fish therefore had to belong in the 6–8lb bracket. You can probably imagine our delight.

Things are a little different when fish are near the surface and then, admittedly, it is easy, in the excitement, to over-estimate what you are watching. This tendency, naturally, is increased many fold if you are watching the fish through binoculars. In fact, field-glasses can make even the smallest roach look a monster. So, when fish are on or near the surface it is a very good idea to try and line them up next to something whose size you are sure about. For example, cut a 12in length of reed and let it float out to the fish you are looking at. Now you have a definite

scale to compare the fish with and it is unlikely that you will be considerably out in your estimations of their size. If this is not possible, wait till the fish move past something that is readily identifiable like a lilypad or they swim underneath a duck even. For that way, again, you get a definite gauge to work out the size of the fish you are watching.

Remember also that the further away from you a fish is swimming the larger it will appear. This is very surprising and I do not know the optical reasons for it but very frequently a monstrous carp at fifty yards will become smaller and smaller until it turns out to be an eight-pounder at the margins. I once made a total fool of myself by becoming wildly excited at the sight of a big bream bow-waving sixty yards from the shore. The bream turned inwards and swam to the bank, where it hopped out and away into the undergrowth looking remarkably like a frog! In low light, at distance, on a glassy, still lake mistakes like this are quite possible and very frustrating.

The fish is in 4ft of water and it is very clear – conditions you would think of as perfect for estimating the weight of a fish. I would have put this particular fish at around 20lb but in fact it was caught later in the season and on the scales went an amazing 27½lb! I am not saying that you can automatically add thirty percent to the weight of a fish you see in such circumstances, but do not rush to judgement without careful consideration.

The start of a winter sequence. The reflections on the water indicate that it is a dark day and the trees have lost all their leaves. In preparation for darkness, which is not far away, the float has a Beta light in it. You may have also noticed, in true detective fashion, the bubbles to the right.

The bubbles are getting much closer now and the float has got rings round it and is beginning to sink.

The fish has got the bait firmly in its mouth and is moving away with it.

Right: And here it is, a beautifully coloured winter carp in the peak of condition.

feeding at some time. As the sun begins to drop, my own excitement rises, as this is a prime time for carp. It seems that they gather momentum throughout the day and then feed steadily as the shadows spread.

It is rare to see winter carp really guzzle food down in the way that summer fish can. Rather they seem to tip up and feed very slowly and very selectively, picking up one or two food items at the most before chewing, whereas in the summer seven or eight can easily disappear into the mouth at once. This habit should encourage the use of fewer and perhaps more obvious baits. After all, what is the use of carpeting the bottom with, say, casters, if only a small percentage are going to be taken. It makes more sense to put out fewer food items so that the bait stands a much greater chance of being taken.

The importance of smell

While we are talking about baits, it is well known that smells are particularly important in the winter and a great deal of time is spent making baits that will release a strong odour in cold water conditions. This is quite important and certainly I have found smells to be a real winter turn-on for carp. You need not be too sophisticated, however. To make one of my favourite winter carp baits I mash bread – yes, bread! – into a bucket, add flavouring and a few bait samples and introduce it in handfuls here and there under trees around the margins. This mix gives a milky, cloudy effect that, combined with the smell, proves very attractive. Carp home in on the baited areas, drawn by both the sight and the smell of the concoction.

Generally, winter tackle can be lighter than the gear you use in the summer. This is fortunate, given that the water is often clearer and carp never lose their caution no matter how cold it becomes. Also, there is less weed for the fish to bury into and so lighter line is acceptable. Lastly, I have found that in winter carp fight in a more sluggish, less dynamic fashion than when water is warmer.

Winter carping is worth the effort and the cold just for the sight of the fish themselves on the bank. You will never see a particular carp look better than it does in winter. The colours of skin and scales really begin to deepen and often a quite pale summer fish will be a burnished gold bronze come the cold season. I have even caught leather carp in the winter that have turned almost a mahogany red.

The flanks of the fish tend to be much firmer in the winter, and are sometimes almost rock-hard. As a result, the fish looks much like a well-conditioned heavyweight boxer – all size, power and muscle; a really majestic sight. However, at this time of year it is also quite common to find small leeches and other parasites clinging to the body of carp. Perhaps because the fish are much more lethargic, this gives parasites a better chance of securing a hold on their host. When I am lucky enough to catch winter carp, I pick off the offending creatures with forceps. I don't know if this does them any good or even whether the leeches do any harm, but it simply reflects the care and love we all feel for this remarkable species.

BARBEL DETECTION

THE FEEDING BARBEL

Watch barbel feeding and you will understand how, when and where they feed and you will be able to catch more. This approach has certainly worked for me, for now I can more than I ever did before I started using it. The way in which barbel feed is not as straightforward as you might think. Clearly those barbules hanging from the mouth are sensitive, like our fingers, and probe the gravel, sand or any other kind of bottom, looking for food particles. So far so good, and frequently you will see puffs of silt appear around the barbel's head as it forages for its dinner.

Equally obvious is the reason for that large, protruding, underslung mouth. The barbel needs to get right up to and even over its food before it can take it into its mouth and is not as adept at sucking food in from a distance as a carp is. (Watch a carp in good detective fashion and you will sometimes see food disappear into its mouth from a good six inches away!)

However, the eyesight of the barbel is far better than you would possibly expect. After all, the eyes do tend to be small and the snout rather big and you would not think they would see very well. On the

Left: This barbel was feeding in water 4ft deep, browsing over a very large rock face and in doing so occasionally disturbing small patches of silt. It was almost certainly looking for caddis grubs, which, since they were clamped onto the stones, took a fair bit of dislodging. From time to time I saw the barbel's tail driving the fish at the caddis like a battering ram in a furious attempt to dislodge a few of them.

Below: If you are observant you may spot 'flashing' barbel – fish that are twisting on the gravel bottom, throwing up clouds of silt and small food items. This activity is exploited by other members of the shoal, which follow close behind, picking out the pieces as the debris falls back to the bottom. Flashing is a useful indicator of feeding, and sometimes a barbel's stomach can be seen gleaming palely through ten or more feet of water.

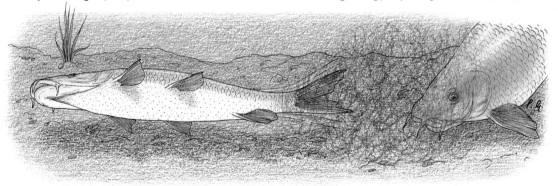

Above: This shot is a bit of a cheat. It certainly shows the flash, like a glowing mirror, that all barbel anglers love to see. However, this is not a barbel feeding on the bottom, but a hooked fish fighting its way towards the net. It is simply because that distinctive mellow-gold flank shows itself to such tremendous advantage that I have included it. You will notice the fish was caught on a cage feeder – a very useful tool in fast-flowing water because it does not catch the current and roll off course.

contrary, every interesting piece of food floating down river is very likely to be seen, intercepted and taken, and this is why freelined baits are often so successful in a river where the fish have become accustomed to static baits fished with a swimfeeder.

Almost equally effective is the barbel's nose. In coloured water it almost certainly hunts by scent and that is when a big, smelly bait like luncheon meat or

Left: Almost certainly British anglers could make much more use of the caddis grub as a bait. Their French counterparts swear by it for barbel in particular. In clean, streamy water you should find the grubs, in their tubes, glued to the underside of fair-sized bricks or stones. It is easy to squeeze them out of the tube and to mount them on a hook suitable for their size. Not surprisingly, all river fish eat caddis in great quantities, for at night the grubs leave their tubes and move around their immediate territory completely unprotected.

A common sight on rivers in the summer and autumn is barbel rolling over a gravel bottom. It is a gentle, confident movement, and you normally see the head, back and dorsal fin, and occasionally the tail fin waving provocatively out of the water. Often this ritual is a prelude to feeding, but do not jump to conclusions, as sometimes barbel will reveal themselves in this way when they are on the move.

cheese really comes into its own. Once visibility is no more than an inch or so there is no way a barbel can either see or feel food easily – it just has to smell it out. This is another bonus for the barbel hunter.

And if those refined senses are not enough, test the barbel's amazing sensitivity to vibration. Watch a small school of barbel from the bank and stamp heavily: not a barbel in sight. The chub might not have gone and the roach will still be there, but the barbel will all have fled. Can this help them feed? Almost certainly. For example, I once saw a large lobworm gyrating near the flank of a feeding barbel. The fish cannot possibly have smelt, felt or seen that worm, but must have sensed it through vibration, whereupon it wheeled round and sucked it in instantly. In short, barbel are perfect all-rounders, well equipped for feeding off the bottom

Big barbel feed quite heavily on fry, mainly gudgeon and other small species, and certainly where barbel are present small fish tend to be in short supply. Keep your eyes open for all the tiny fish that scatter in panic as barbel enter the swim.

This striking formation occurs where the current hits the bank and gouges out soft material. The process continues until the undercut is so deep that the bank above it collapses. Barbel and chub love these underwater caverns and will often spend all day there, tempted out only by the cover of darkness or, in daylight, by a mass of bait deposited just outside their haven.

and in some more unexpected places, as we shall see.

Under normal circumstances barbel tend to work slowly upstream, sucking up food as they cover the gravel. Frequently a shoal will move in quite strict regimentation, presenting a very imposing sight indeed, and a thrilling one if your bait is in their path. However, this steady, confident march will very soon be interrupted if the barbel are frightened in any way at all, for then they will turn, allowing the current to catch their bodies, and wheel away to sanctuary. The barbel suddenly becomes a surging, powerful giant and you can see now the force of that first run, which must be contained if the barbel is to be kept from snags.

The flashing barbel is a feeding barbel, for whatever reason, as, in many cases, is a rolling one. So too, generally, is any barbel that looks alert – one swinging in and out of weed fronds, for example.

Daylight feeding

We all know barbel feed in the hours of darkness. Certainly they prowl a good deal once darkness has fallen, often leaving their daytime hang-outs and covering quite large areas of river. Yet they will feed happily in the daytime, provided there is enough shelter over the swim to subdue light – trees most commonly serve this purpose. But there are significant exceptions. In March 1993 I was fishing a low, clear river. A harsh, bright sun was beating on the shallows, but barbel were there, backs out, feeding hard. Six fish were

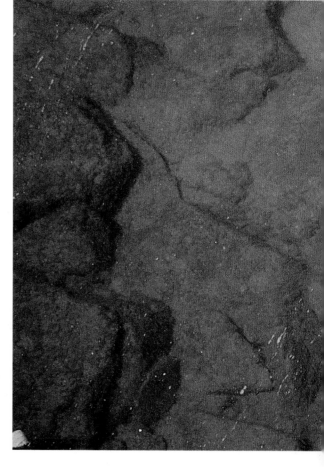

Barbel and gravel form such a natural partnership that you will seldom find a barbel feeding over any other bottom material. In a few rivers gravel is scarce and there they might browse over a clear bottom, but observation bears out the fact that they are most at home when their barbules are working through loose stones and gravel.

Below: A feeding barbel of 5–6lb twists under a rock in bright sunlight, reflecting back a beautiful gleam. Very vigorous feeders, barbel will investigate every nook and cranny in their search for sustenance.

As a result of summer rain the river is 4ft up from its normal level and beginning to run very coloured. It will be like this for another twenty-four hours, but as the water fines down the barbel will almost certainly begin to feed very hard and continue to do so for the next two or three days.

caught in two, bright days when all other swims proved useless both by day and night. Barbel, then, are creatures of shade by preference but not by rule.

It is probably fair to say that the better you can see barbel – that is, the clearer the water – the more important the question of light will become. After rain, when the river is running high and coloured, daylight becomes a less important element in the feeding programme. In winter, when the river runs like soup, light or at least half-light is probably a better proposition than darkness.

Dropping temperatures are bad news for both the barbel and his pursuer. Once the river edges towards 4–5°C (39–41°F) or below, the fish become notice-

ably disinclined to feed, especially when these temperatures are allied, as they usually are, to high pressure, clear skies and low, crystal-clear water. If the weather has been stable, even though cold, for a while, you might stand a chance as the barbel get used to conditions they do not really like. At such times, though, you will often see them looking pretty dismal and unresponsive. They will lie there like logs on the bottom with hardly a flicker of those delightful coral fins. But if there is as much as a hint of a westerly wind,

warm rain and a rising thermometer, the whole situation can change dramatically overnight.

At the other end of the thermometer, I am not really sure what conclusions to draw. Extreme heat can make fishing and feeding sluggish, but a good old storm perks the fish up wonderfully. In the real dogdays of high summer very early morning can see the heaviest period of barbel feeding of all the twenty-four hours. A thermometer reveals that the water temperature is at its lowest around dawn, and especially if

Above: A huge barbel has come in from the main current to browse around some large boulders where it knows large items of food will be available for it. The fish is about fifteen yards from the bank and would easily merge in with the stones and be missed were it not for the pale orange fins that stand out quite clearly from the general background of brown.

there is a heavy dew, you are likely to see barbel move onto the shallows frequently and begin some intense feeding before switching off almost entirely for the rest of the day.

The traditional 'tabletop' will be clean gravel, sand or stones where the barbel can forage for the small food items that infest such areas. They will probably even seek out larger ones, such as bullheads, loach and crayfish. But barbel have more up their sleeves than that and can prove the most enterprising of feeders. Indeed they are able to utilize a wide range of feeding surfaces. The Parlour Pool on the Hampshire Avon's Royalty fishery, is an interesting example. Where the water runs into the pool itself, barbel always hang,

holding position in the middle of the fast water and hoovering the wall of the weir itself for silkweed and the insects that cling to it. In fact, the barbel here at least behave much more like chub and suggest the surprising versatility of the species.

Amazingly, overhanging rocks present no problem to barbel either. They can turn upside down and hold position in the fastest water while hoovering the underneath of rocks, efficiently sucking in caddis that are clinging there in apparent safety.

In short, what we have is a lively, aware fish that feeds across a wide temperature range, in most conditions, on many foodstuffs, off many surfaces and in a variety of ways. A hell of a fella, the barbel!

Right: This picture not only shows the dramatic flash of feeding barbel well but also proves that they will feed upside down in very fast water. This really takes some doing, and for this and many other remarkable skills I have come to respect barbel more and more over the years.

WYE INVESTIGATION

For an investigation into barbel that I carried out on 28 June 1993 I chose a section of the middle Wye. Three factors determined my choice. The first is that I have known this mile-long stretch quite intimately for seven or eight years in all conditions. Secondly, it is an ideal piece of water to merit an exercise of this sort as it displays virtually every major feature a thinking angler could want to fathom out. Finally, this is an important salmon beat, so the barbel and the chub are not unduly affected by coarse-fishing pressure. This means that they act rather more naturally than is the case on some very heavily bombarded stretches of, say, the Wessex rivers.

The stretch really starts with what might appear to be quite a dull, placid strait. At first sight, there seems to be nothing special about the area at all. However, if you use the evidence carefully, you will see that one or two interesting things emerge. First of all, about a hundred yards upstream on the far bank, some very large pieces of rubble have been shipped into the river to strengthen the crumbling clay banks. These large boulders and pieces of masonry have given the barbel a great deal of shelter and food and at least two or three shoals have been drawn into the area. The rubble area itself is very difficult to fish, if not usually impossible, but this does not matter, as the fish do move freely for at least two hundred yards upstream and downstream of this prime point.

Barbel and chub lairs

This is where our bank comes in. Many years ago a large groyne was built out at the tail of the run to allow salmon anglers better access over the water. It has long since collapsed but the foundation stones have withstood the force of many winter floods and over the years have provided a tremendous attraction for moving barbel. In this low, clear water it is very easy to see the lie of the brickwork and mentally position baits for coming sessions when spotting conditions might not be so kind.

From there, the glide quickens considerably, the river narrows and the Wye shoots into a quarter of a mile of gravels, rapids, deep holes and long areas of streamer weed. Both chub and barbel adore this particular area, especially in the summer. The gravel

This photograph shows the old stones of the groyne very clearly. To get the shot I had to wait some time for the water to be low enough and clear enough, as well as for the sun to be at the right angle I wanted. Rest assured that in the winter the piece of river just out from these stones makes a tremendous holding place for some very big fish.

MONSTERS

Anybody familiar with the writings of several well-known anglers in the 1950s and 1960s might remember that they swore to the presence of huge barbel in the middle Avon, fish whose weight they put at 15–20lb. At the time, and since then to some extent, it has been fashionable to count these sightings as wishful thinking and typical of the overexuberance of that period.

However, in the distant past, huge barbel have been recorded, including seventeen-pounders on the Trent and one of 20lb from the Thames. Just because these are old records it does not mean to say that they are necessarily false and it could be that the upper limit of barbel in this country is higher than we realize. Come to that, we do actually have a photograph of a barbel of 16lb 1oz held by the famous Ibsley water bailiff Lt Col S. H. Crowe which was foul-hooked by a salmon fisherman on the Hampshire Avon. Here is the proof, if only in black and white.

More recently, rumours have been rife about huge fish – and we are talking about massive specimens – in stretches of the River Severn. I have also heard of a 17lb Wye barbel, again foul-hooked by a salmon angler. Could it be then that these monsters – which would be far larger than the British record barbel – are out there still waiting to be caught?

Dreams play their part, even in the cold, logical world of detection. Hopes of a fantastic fish are often needed to drag us out night after cold night. But are such fish there? The evidence suggests that they are, or at least a few fish between 16lb and perhaps 18lb. Why are they not caught then, ask the cynics? Could it be that these super-barbel somehow turn away from normal baits and become immune to normal tactics? Perhaps they have become confirmed fish eaters? Why, the cynics chime, do river-pike anglers not take them from time to time? Perhaps these massive barbel, inevitably many years old, are just too clever to pick up baits festooned with treble hooks and wire.

If these fish exist, say the sceptics again, then why has no one caught even the occasional fish of over 16lb during the past half century? Surely ill luck cannot dog every barbel angler all his life on every session. Strange, I freely admit, but I suspect that one night an angler out there on the Severn, probably in early March, when the fish will be at its heaviest, will strike into one of these barbel around which fables have grown up. Until such a time, sadly, it is impossible to separate fact from fantasy.

Below left: This submerged punt has quite a history. It might not look much at all but underneath it a 14lb barbel was once caught! The more you think about it the more obvious it is why this swim should appeal to a big fish. Note how the water sweeps over the remains of an old wall. The rocks are still clearly visible and offer both food and protection from the quick current. Then there is the punt itself, often cloaked with caddis and small snails as well as providing shade from the sun and welcome respite from the current.

Above: If you are after large barbel you should get yourself a big landing net and always remember that the battle is not over until the fish is on the bank. See how the angler is passing the net's pole through his hands so that he can grasp the mesh and frame before turning back to come onto the bank.

Right: No less than any other species, the barbel deserves respect and should held over an unhooking mat before its final return. That way, even if it should wriggle free it will have a soft fall and can be retrieved and held head first in the current until it recovers.

A great sweep of ranunculus weed – much frequented by barbel throughout the summer. Often you have to watch very closely indeed in order to catch sight of the fish beneath the waving fronds.

harbours abundant food for the fish, while the streamer weed provides shelter from bright, summer sunlight and some protection from the heavy currents. Also, there is no doubt that both species enjoy rubbing themselves on the stones and it is possible to sit watching their sides glinting as they turn and the flash of scales attracts the sunlight. The old theory was that fish were cleaning themselves after spawning, but I cannot agree.

Most commonly, a flashing fish, either a chub or a barbel, is regarded as a feeding fish and this certainly is often the case. Anybody who keeps gudgeon in a tank will see that they rub the gravel with their shoulders and flanks only to turn and sift through the silt as it falls back again. There is no doubt that both chub and barbel do this, the one fish helping the shoal member immediately behind it. However, I am not convinced that either of these suggestions is the whole and only truth. My own feeling is that while the feeding explanation is very often right, the fish may go through this manoeuvre to rid themselves of an annoying parasite.

Freelining a natural bait

Though the fish certainly inhabit this fast water in numbers, it is not easy to present bait to them in a totally convincing fashion by any standard method. Even with a swimfeeder, loose feed tends to get swept many yards downstream and the fish, if hungry, disperse and go hunting after it. A far better idea is to trundle a large natural bait such as a lobworm or two, or a large slug, down through the runs in the streamer weed with perhaps one or two SSG shot 12–18in up the line. Here a long rod is useful for better control and the line should not be less than 6–7lb b.s. The new, thin co-polymer lines from Japan are excellent for this job as they are less visible to the fish and, with their narrower diameter, less likely to be caught by the current.

It really does pay to watch the water on an area like this and stalk patiently until the silver gleams of twisting fish are seen. Of course, it is not always as easy as this. On the day of my investigation, for example, the sun was so bright that most fish were inhibited from showing themselves at all. Even so, at such times there are still some good opportunities for the angler who uses his eyes. The force of the current on that stretch of the river is such that very frequently the bank is eaten away and seriously undercut caverns have appeared very close to the bank. Both barbel and chub (as well as salmon) love to use these. Again, they have

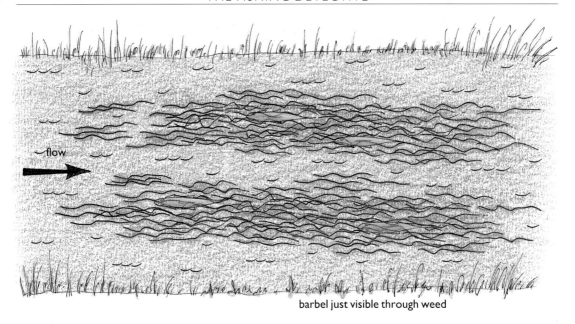

flow

barbel just visible through weed

Above: Security is of prime importance to barbel, and if they cannot find a deep hole or an undercut bank they will usually lie under fronds of streamer weed. Watch these carefully and when they sway in the current it is just possible that you will spot the indistinct outline of a barbel within them. Very often, though, all you will see is a moving tail or a pectoral fin.

Below: One of the most unusual barbel swims I have ever seen is on the River Wye. The fish haunt the carcass of a drowned cow, whose remains break up the current. They weave in and out of the ribcage, sometimes venturing into the flow and sometimes drifting with it along the backbone. It is a gruesome yet effective reminder that barbel like to frequent snags of all kinds.

shelter from bright light and the full force of the current. Also, the current brings constant food into their underwater stronghold. These are excellent swims and when the sun is at its brightest it pays to spend a good hour watching for signs of the odd fishy feature protruding out of the overhang into open water.

We now come to a very important group of swims. We have moved on from the extreme rapids and the river has slowed down but still has a good pace to it. Moreover, it is channelled sharply into our bank, cutting away the clay in a series of overhangs. There are some large fallen trees that give added protection and confidence and finally, trees (mainly alder, oak and ash)

In the bottom left-hand part of the photograph you can see quite clearly a clay ridge that runs out into the river. This falls away very suddenly into 10ft of water and is undercut at the bottom where it meets the gravel. In fact, I have been in to investigate and found that the undercut actually tunnels 3–4ft back under the bank – a marvellous den for barbel.

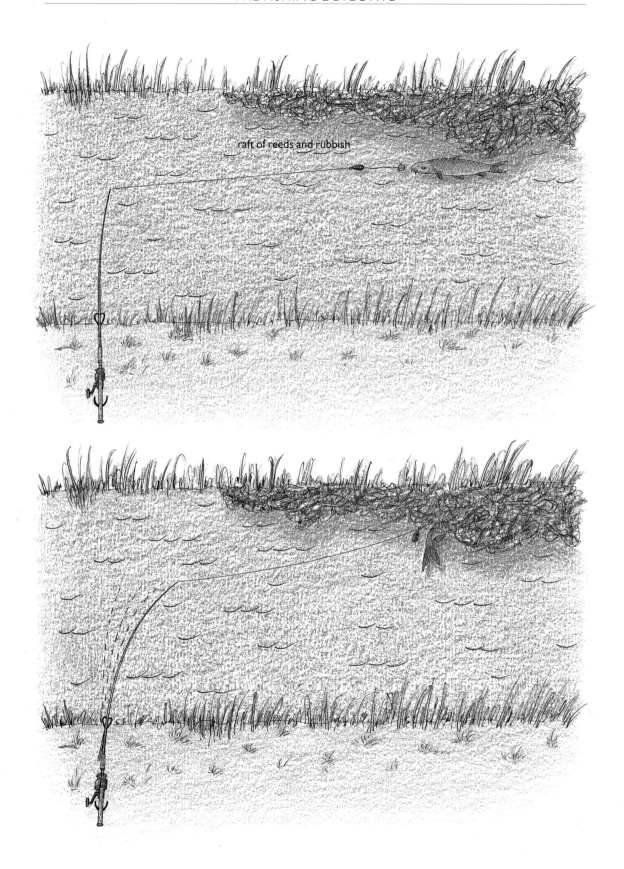

raft of reeds and rubbish

Left: A bait placed next to a snag will often provoke a fearsome bite from a barbel, which slips out from safety, grabs the bait and then flees as fast as it can back to where it came from. Bites like this bend the rod right round and you must react very rapidly if you are to prevent the fish from regaining its snaggy sanctuary.

Below: In case you are wondering, my own shadow is in the photograph to give some idea of the scale. You will notice at once several things. First, look at the enormous marooned tree stump that provides excellent protection for the barbel. Second, right by my elbow, a clay outcrop juts out into the river, its underneath hollowed away to provide a haven that often holds a couple of fish. Third, above my head you will see the dense shadow of a large tree. Barbel particularly like shade and in fact there were five or six fish feeding there, hidden from the light, at that very moment. They actually follow the shadow around the swim as the sun moves. Finally, notice the bottom of the swim. Clean gravel and sand and small stones, it is just what this bottom-feeding species favours. All in all, a perfect barbel swim in a single frame.

overhang the water in many places, giving shade from the sun from around one o'clock onwards.

This package of features is extremely inviting and barbel often come on the feed in these swims from the mid or late afternoon onwards, even under bright conditions. For at least a quarter of a mile, the river does nothing particularly interesting. Its pace is diminishing all the time and it grows wider and featureless. True, in the winter especially, the odd very big fish takes residence for a short while close in to the bank, under some tree or another, but the odds against finding one are too great to make it worthwhile trying.

We turn a right-handed bend as we go downstream and another set of gravels confronts us. Both barbel and chub do come from this area but it is nowhere near the most successful of quicker-water reaches. In part, detective work seems to suggest that there are not enough overhanging trees on either bank and the bed itself is so consistently gravel that

There is no disputing the fact that snags and barbel go together. This raft has been in existence for well over five years and now has an almost resident shoal of fish beneath it.

weed finds it very hard to grow there. The result is that there is very little shelter for any larger fish.

This is not the case just a hundred yards downstream. Here the main current hits a steeply wooded bank and moves off to the left. This area might appear quite nondescript but the detective knows better. The great height of the trees keeps the sun off the water virtually all day and although the swims are uniformly shallow, with few snags or weed, barbel and chub seek the shade for many hours of the day. In fact, they can often be seen browsing on the stones, hunting out caddis, small crayfish and snails.

This is very much the stalking man's water. An ideal approach is to put a dozen or so handfuls of corn in where they can be seen. It is then a case of waiting and watching until something begins to move onto the patches. For four hundred yards, the river then does nothing in particular but meanders a slow solemn way until it reaches a very large willow where over many years a thick raft has built up that not even the most vicious of winter floods can disperse. This is the only traditional barbel swim on the entire stretch. Barbel and rafts, everybody knows, go together and this swim is no exception. There are generally barbel at home winter and summer. The interesting thing is that the barbel have completely claimed this swim for themselves and it is very rare for chub to get a look in. Indeed, probably only one fish in ten is a chub, so complete is the dominance of barbel in this prime swim.

The angling detective now knows only too well why a raft should be such a magnet. The reason is simply that, winter or particularly summer, it acts as a ceiling against the bright, sunlit world above and neither barbel nor big chub go together with light.

A CHANCE OCCURRENCE

A little way upstream of a favourite barbel swim of mine was an old road bridge, built originally for pack animals and horse-drawn vehicles. Its age made the structure fragile and with little effort pieces could be prized off the top. The local boys knew this and the temptation to remove pieces of masonry was always great. That, I suspect, is how quite a large piece of the bridge found itself in this excellent swim, opposite a tangle of willow trees about a hundred yards or so downstream.

This shot pinpoints a barbel hotspot some ten yards from the bank, to where I waded out with the camera halfway through a session. You will see that a great deal of sweetcorn (a hookbait in use) has gathered around a large rock. The current has swept it along and deposited it in that one location and that is where the barbel have been sweeping in to feed. During the first part of the session I had taken three fish by putting a bait almost exactly there (though not knowing the reason) whereas my friend fishing five yards away had remained biteless.

Before long the detective in me realized that the water was pushed up over the lump of masonry and then swirled down behind, creating a small depression in the river bed. Little by little the barbel had become used to finding this depression, which was attractive to them because it provided shelter behind the rubble and also because food began to collect there. In fact, it was quite possible to see bait and items such as dead minnows rise over the masonry and be pulled down by the currents into the depression behind it.

The more the barbel fed there, the deeper the hole became and the more food collected. More food meant more barbel and a deeper depression, and soon the only place to put a bait in the entire swim was in this particular hole. Provided you got a bait in there – and it really did not matter very much what it was – you would be sure to get a bite sooner or later. Since then I have seen, and enjoyed, many another barbel swim created similarly by mere chance.

THERMOMETERS

You might think that anything which gathers clues to help detection would be welcomed and half of me says that thermometers are really valuable tools for this purpose. Indeed, throughout most of the 1970s I had one with me all the time and would nearly always take water temperature readings whenever I went roach fishing. The conclusions were interesting but never totally satisfying and very often fish fed when they should not have done, or did not when they should have – all very baffling and rather annoying. As a result, around about 1980, this particular fishing detective laid aside his thermometer for good.

A mistake? Maybe it was. Recently I fished with a party of anglers on an autumn river where the going for barbel was very difficult indeed. The water temperatures had dropped like a stone and at the start of the week were hovering around 4°C (39°F). It was too cold, we

all knew, for barbel. All the books have said so and who were we to disagree?

However, a couple of the party continued to take water readings and even though air temperatures did not appear to change much, the water gradually began to warm. Most significantly, it was discovered that the water temperature appeared to be at its highest around dusk. Now, we all know that barbel like to feed as the light fades but perhaps this is linked with warmer water. Anyway, the results of these readings meant that we all fished with renewed optimism and vigour as darkness approached and, sure enough, four out of the five barbel that rewarded us that week were caught at last light or just into darkness.

Where does that leave me? Being serious about detection, perhaps I ought to go back to my thermometer and once again take accurate reading whenever I possibly can.

It was an interesting day weather-wise when this shot was taken. Until mid afternoon it had been bright and clear, with a brisk wind, but around four o'clock cloud began to appear, it grew muggy and the wind died away almost completely. A disappointing day suddenly became golden in terms of fish caught and the next two hours saw four barbel on the bank. Had the fish detected some change in the atmospheric pressure or was it the difference in light that provoked a feeding spell? It remains an open question but constant observation eventually solves many riddles of this sort.

BARBEL FORTNIGHT

During the last two weeks in August, a group of a dozen anglers fished the River Wye in the tail-end of a very erratic summer. Throughout that fortnight the river was progressively dropping and clearing and initially water temperatures were dropping too. For the first few days the barbel proved very difficult indeed and only a few were landed. Those that were caught were liberally covered in water fleas – normally a problem that only afflicts fish in the winter when water temperatures are low and the fish are moving very little. Could the water fleas be a clue? Were water temperatures so low and was the water so clear that the barbel here were hardly moving at all, thereby leaving themselves vulnerable to infestation?

During that first part of the fortnight, the only place that barbel were caught with any regularity was in one

This barbel fell to swimfeeder-fished maggots in the deep hole that can be seen in the background. This is a splendid swim and offers several benefits to the barbel: depth, shelter from floods and a hard, rocky bottom to feed over. Generally they are smaller school fish, like this six-pounder, but from time to time the odd very big barbel moves in.

of the deepest, current-riddled pools. There a large shoal of fish had gathered, still willing to feed. Ninety percent of the fish that were caught during that period came from this one area.

As the days went by, the situation changed, however. The sun began to shine again and temperatures rose. The new light and increased clarity meant that barbel could be observed far more clearly in other points of the river. There were barbel by the bridge, there were barbel by the stump, there were barbel in the shallows – there seemed to be barbel just about everywhere. And they were active creatures, frequently flashing and constantly jostling for position in the swim. The very notion of comatose fish could now be laughed at as a joke. But the fish were no easier to catch, for all that. While it was possible to see shoals of barbel rising and twisting and apparently feeding, to hook one seemed a virtual impossibility.

What were the options and what were the explanations? At times so frantic was the barbels' behaviour that it almost appeared that spawning was continuing. However, the lateness of the year and the depressed water temperatures seemed to completely rule this

out. Surely the fish were catchable. Some anglers tried a matchman's approach – very light hooks, gossamer hooklengths and liberal feeding with small baits, especially maggots, casters and hemp. But still very little was caught, although one small fish was hooked and lost beneath the bridge, the light tackle proving to be completely inadequate. So what next?

Like a fairy tale, a partial answer came right out of the blue. It had been noticeable that wherever there were barbel there seemed to be a total absence of any small fish. There appeared to be some correlation too clear to ignore. Were the barbel simply scaring fry, minnows, gudgeon and so on from their areas or were they actually predators?

While all this was going through my mind, a baby gudgeon inexplicably rose to the surface and swam to the edge near my feet, where it wriggled limply against the bank. I had never seen this happen before and I think I was probably as stunned as the tiny fish itself. All the same, I knelt and caught it quite easily in my hand. I presumed it had been wounded in some way but providence seemed too generous to ignore. I killed the small fish and retackled, impaling it on a size 6 hook. I cast to where I knew there were barbel and within two minutes had a bite that all but ripped the rod from my hands. The gudgeon had been stripped from the hook and I had not hit anything on the strike.

Nevertheless, a possible answer had emerged, and over the next few days I used minnows and small gudgeon extensively, landing five barbel and losing two more as well as missing another handful of bites. All this was very encouraging. Now, I am not saying that this single lesson has revolutionized barbel fishing: that would be crazy but that fortnight's experience really did stretch the mind and, I believe, produced a partial solution to the problem of very difficult barbel.

Left: A perfect barbel area. Notice how a deep hole begins to shallow out and run quickly over gravel and larger stones. Over a three-day period this particular run provided almost twenty fish of over 10lb.

Right: Barbel and sunset are a combination that has long been recognized. This fish was just over 10lb and took three casters on a size 14 hook. It fought so hard that I thought the sun would be gone altogether by the time it was landed.

BARBEL HOLES

Where do barbel like to live? There is no doubt in my mind that bottom contours and particularly hidden, underwater snags play a huge role in barbel location. Rafts, snags and fallen trees are perhaps a part of the answer in smaller rivers such as the Wensum or the Suffolk Stour, but on larger rivers the situation is far more complicated. For example, on the Thames there is very little surface indication of a barbel lie and every clue has to be examined. There, underwater contours are invisible and can only really be discovered by the most accurate plumbing techniques.

Locating barbel

On a clearer spate river like the Wye or the Severn you can visit when the river is dead, rock-bottom low, and pick up valuable pointers to barbel location. At such times you will often see in mid-stream a sunken tree, a pile of rubble, an old, discarded piece of farm machinery or even the skeleton of some unfortunate beast from the Welsh mountains; any of these indicate a prime barbel swim for the future. On all barbel rivers,

in high-water conditions and resultant poor visibility, a boat and a graph recorder have in many cases provided the same type of information to build upon.

One definite fact that investigator after investigator has picked up for at least a century is that there are barbel holes. By this I mean particular places on all rivers that have always attracted the species. The Trent Otter talked about these holes a century ago and certainly they exist on completely unfished stretches of the Wye, so they have nothing really to do with anglers' baits. 'Holes' has got to be the right word for the swims I am talking about, for they nearly always exist where there is a real dip, often unexpected, in a river bed. Once you have located one, you will find barbel. Not just once, not just for a week or two, but always. I know half a dozen or so holes on the Wye and more on the Wensum and it does not matter when I fish them – high water, low water, summer or winter – barbel are there. It brings to mind the way badgers keep to a particular sett generation after generation, only moving if a disaster befalls them.

There is more to the investigation, of course. Current speed and direction seem to play a very important part in determining where barbel like to live. In fact, there are certain occasions when current speed plays a very obvious role. For example, during a strong

Below: Many rivers have swims based on a hollow in the bed where barbel reside all year round, seemingly never moving far away. In years gone by a good number of writers commented on this habit and the term 'barbel hole' has been in use for at least a century. In these depressions the current is less aggressive and so the barbel can relax. A further advantage is that food is pushed down into these slack areas, so that finding food is not a problem. On either side of the hole there are often shallow gravel runs, perfect areas for the barbel when it wants to come out of its hole to feed in the relative safety of dusk or dawn.

Right: A barbel lies beaten before the hole where it lives and from where it was caught. Look at the shape of this fish: it was late summer and it was feeding very hard before the first frosts of the autumn would slow it down. For this reason, September is often a golden period for the big-barbel hunter.

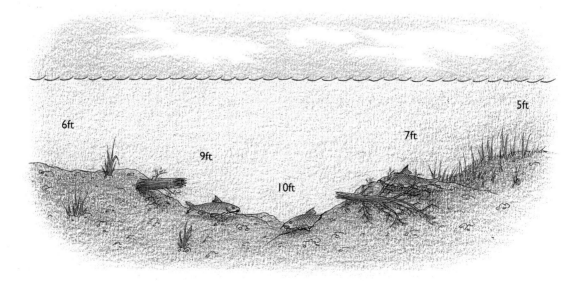

Left: Barbel adore this run of water, here seen from a road bridge. Actually, the pool was created by salmon anglers in the past and now the water is channelled to some extent between large rocks. This has increased the flow of the water and barbel love it, spending long periods in the quicker stretch before dropping downstream some twenty or thirty yards to where the water slows down and deepens. Barbel often favour this type of area, feeding in the faster water and resting not far away where it is more relaxed.

flood we all know that barbel will move out from the margins and linger in eddies and slacks. Again, in times of very low water they will also look for any current whatsoever to give them a push of oxygen.

It is general conditions that are the problem. I know the ideal current speed when I see it but how do I describe it on paper? Come to think of it, the ideal current cannot be judged on its speed alone – there is something more to it: the look of the water. How crinkly is it? How steadily paced? Does it boil at all? A lot? Too much?

As for current direction, I feel barbel like to face it head on but also they will look out for slight deflections over weeds, round parapets and so on. On big rivers,

on the few occasions when you can see the fish, it is interesting to note that not all of them lie with their heads facing the current, many preferring to take up an oblique angle to it. Again, I am not clear about the reason for this, but it could be that the current direction is altered and manipulated at the bottom of the river and does not flow in quite the way we expect, judging from the surface.

I have known some barbel holes in my life but never one to compete with the one I am going to describe. The river upstream of it covers two hundred yards of extremely fast, gravelly rapids and then slows, deepens and turns a very long right-handed bend before shallowing out again to the next set of rapids. This bend is about sixty to seventy yards long, ten yards

Below: This is a very big barbel – over 11lb – that was caught from a hole where I had expected school fish of no more than 6–7lb to be living. In fact, this fish was never seen again in the hole even though it is fished very frequently. Almost certainly we had just chanced lucky and hit it as it was perhaps spending the odd day with its younger cousins. The sun was setting, as is often the case when you take a good barbel, and gave the fish its beautiful golden glow.

wide and up to twenty feet deep – though this last factor obviously varies.

Now, I happen to know, because I have caught them on a few occasions, that there are barbel that live in this hole probably most of their lives. The area has everything they could possibly want. In the spring, they can move upstream or downstream to spawn in the shallows. In the summer they can hunt minnows, small fry, bullheads and all manner of aquatic creatures on the quicker gravelly runs just above and below the

hole. When the water gets cold or clear they can settle into the depth of the hole, and when it rises in flood there are plenty of slacks and eddies just to the side of the area to provide shelter.

In short, this hole is the perfect environment, for the barbel need never go travelling at all. This does not mean that new barbel do not arrive now and again. In fact, when conditions are right, groups of very big fish will stay in the hole for quite a while – generally throughout the winter.

Failing to anticipate the deep, powerful, boring run of a barbel, this angler has not given out line. As a result his rod has been pulled down parallel to the water, so that the fish is on a dangerously short tight line and may well either break him or shake free of the hook.

Naturally, I am not the only one to have found out about this hole over the years and it gets a fair amount of pressure from anglers. As a result, the fish have become wary. Bites can be very shy indeed and it certainly pays to think hard about baits and presentation. For example everybody uses a swimfeeder. Try a lead! Everybody fishes a static bait. Try float fishing, just tripping the bait along the bottom! Everybody uses maggot, caster or sweetcorn. Try a lobworm, a dead minnow or even a large lump of cheese. Everybody tends to fish the deepest part of the hole itself. Try, perhaps, fishing the head or the tail of the hole in the early morning or later on at night when it is very likely that the barbel begin to spill out of the deepest water to forage for food.

This is simply one of those cases when you know the barbel are there and it is up to you to break away from a handful of set approaches of which the fish have obviously become extremely suspicious, to make sure that you actually get them out.

The angler has made a misjudgement as he brings the barbel to the net. His rod is as far back as it will go and still the barbel is not within range. This is a risky time and he is very likely to have to give some slack line, which could result in the hook slipping. He will now have to put down the net, change the rod back to his right hand and reel in 4–5ft of line before he can try again – altogether an unwelcome manoeuvre to embark on at this crucial stage in the fight.

WHEN THE MINNOWS GO

Picture a steady, deepish swim that flows over gravel and underneath alder and willow trees. You begin with maggots and casters and a block-end feeder and for half an hour suffer from a constant barrage of tweaking minnows. The quivertip is simply never still as soon as the bait hits the bottom. Then, after about the twentieth cast, things become a little more sane. The maggots can stay out for a good five minutes without coming back chewed beyond recognition. After around seventy minutes there seems to be no minnow activity whatsoever. Things are getting interesting! At the hour-and-a-half mark, quite suddenly after ten minutes of complete peace, the tip thwacks round and you are suddenly playing a barbel.

This scenario happens repeatedly and almost certainly the minnows are shouldered aside as barbel begin to infiltrate the swim, probably attracted both by the maggots and by the frenzied minnows' activity itself. Much the same goes for chub: once the barbel have muscled in, they will likewise be shouldered aside.

The moral is that it is worth waiting, for the pecking order eventually asserts itself. All you have to do then is catch the barbel!

A magical stretch of river in France. In general about 4ft deep, the water runs steadily towards the distant mill, moving over gravel and through streamer weed. The river is infested with small fish such as gudgeon, bleak and minnows and it is abundantly clear how predatory the barbel are. In the early morning, when this photograph was taken, shoals of fish can often be seen sweeping in from deeper water and attacking fry along the shallows. The locals know this and fish for the barbel with small livebaits under floats, drifting down the current.

TWO BARBEL CASE STUDIES

For our first case study, let us imagine you are using maggots, say two or three on a size 12 or 14 hook. You are getting bites on the quivertip but nothing very definite and those that you have struck at you have missed. What is going on? Study the maggots for a possible clue. Suppose that maggots are nibbled extensively at their tails and almost certainly small fry or minnows are responsible. They are simply getting from the maggot what they can without being large enough to take them firmly in their mouth.

However, suppose you are missing the bites and the maggots are coming back just slightly flattened, but not really crushed at all. This is far more interesting, indicating a larger fish showing some interest but without yet giving a really positive bite. What can you do? Perhaps scaling down to two maggots on a size 16 might provoke a response. However, you should not go too light because barbel are powerful fish.

Gaining the barbel's confidence

Alternatively, you might wait for the light to dim a bit. If the culprits are barbel then almost certainly the bites will become more forceful and easy to hit as evening approaches. Then again, you could try edging the bait slightly closer to some snag or to some area where you think the barbel might feed with a little more confidence. If you are presenting a bite in the middle of open water, they might be approaching the maggots with temerity and not really risking engulfing them too far away from sanctuary.

Do you strike at relatively small bites or do you wait for the tip to really go round? Traditionally, barbel anglers do the latter but not all barbel bite as though they would hang themselves. The trouble is that if you strike at too many twitches unsuccessfully, a feeder or a bomb bouncing around the swim is only likely to unsettle the barbel even more and make bites even gentler or even make them stop altogether. Perhaps a balance needs to be struck. Wait for a big bite but if any knock looks more definite, give it a try.

And what about line bites? We all know to expect these from bream, say, but barbel? A barbel is a big fish and it moves vigorously around the bottom, often using the current to sweep it rapidly several feet over the gravel. It is obviously likely to brush your line during these excursions and what frequently indicates this is a sharp nod at the rod tip, which is over and back again in a split second. Do not try to hit these, because you are likely to simply scare fish or, even worse, foulhook them. Wait for something more positive.

For the second case study I must go back to one morning in 1979 when I was watching a piece of luncheon meat (not attached to hook or line) that was lying on a stretch of gravel just outside a raft serving as home to a 9lb barbel. The fish appeared first of all around ten o'clock and looked very definitely at the meat. Equally definitely it turned away. A hour later the procedure was repeated, only this time the barbel inched a little closer before ultimately rejecting it.

To cut a very long story short, that barbel visited the meat five times over three and a half hours. Only after this protracted inspection did it take it – and then with obvious reluctance. What happened was this: the barbel edged up to the meat, lay for two minutes with its nose pressed to it and then, in a lightning movement, sucked it in and swept back under the tree roots to safety. Had that meat been on a hook then the rod tip would have moved two feet in no time at all.

Now, this story shows why I believe so many barbel bites are really ferocious on many rivers. The barbel is by no means a stupid fish and it certainly recognizes dangerous food and dangerous situations, and when greed gets the upper hand panic still sets in at the crucial moment. How many times do you hear of a rod tip swinging round wildly, or reels screeching at the bite or even of gear being dragged into the river? My detective work leads me to think that all this is a result of frightened fish that have been under pressure.

Fearless feeders

Take a different case. It is 1993 and I am on a stretch of river that has probably never been coarse fished at all. The swim is a large, deep one of moderate pace and barbel roll from time to time in sufficient numbers to indicate that a shoal is present. During the day three of them are landed, but not once does the tip move more than a couple of inches and on one occasion you would simply have thought a butterfly was passing and brushing the rod with its wings, so feeble was the movement. In this case, reason says that the barbel simply mooched up to the bait, took it in and proceeded to eat it on the spot without fear.

Most barbel bites fall somewhere between these two extremes and come from fish which are only averagely aware and only half afraid. Even so the mental state of the barbel you are seeking can be read from what they do to the rod tip.

I struck at the most minute flick on the rod tip, which I would not normally do, and found myself attached to a very big fish. You will see how my left hand is supporting the rod a little way up from the butt. This is important in that it gives more power and leverage and helps prise a big fish from the bottom.

PREDATOR DETECTION

THE FEEDING PIKE

How does a pike feed? This is an important question that the fishing detective must address if he is to understand how and why he catches pike at all. The basics are comparatively simple. A pike lies virtually comatose somewhere in the water. If this is a shallow stillwater or Broad, for example, then it will probably rest on the bottom, probably cradled by reeds or fallen branches. But if the water is a deep Scottish loch, then the pike will probably hang somewhere deep down, possibly on the edge of the thermocline, that area where the warmer water plunges away into a void of cold depth.

There the pike lies while its last meal is being digested. Depending on the size of the pike, the warmth of the water and the size of the meal, this process may last several days before hunger again begins to make itself felt. As the desire to eat increases so the pike becomes more alert. Soon this alertness becomes noticeable action and the pike begins to move in search of prey.

There are probably two main ways in which the pike hunts. First, it may lie largely hidden around an area it knows is frequented by prey fish, ambushing an

A perfect ambush area for pike: a large bay of around thirty acres lying just off a major Scottish loch. The water is 2–10ft deep and heavily festooned with reeds and even lilies. The bay is used most between March and May as a spawning ground but big pike come in from time to time in search of small ones or wandering groups of trout. It is also a perfect area for pike to lie low and digest their food.

unsuspecting fish as it moves past close enough to be attacked. Alternatively the pike goes off on the prowl, looking for a large shoal of prey fish. If the shoal is large enough and perhaps preoccupied with feeding, the predator might well think its chances of an open attack are relatively high and will strike into it, making fish leap and scatter in all directions.

Mysteries of the pike

When the pike catches a fish it holds it across its mouth with its needle-sharp teeth while the lifeblood drains from it. As the prey's struggles cease and the chances of escape disappear, the pike will turn it and swallow it head first. The digestion process then begins once again and a whole cycle repeats itself that will continue over and over until death. This is only an outline, and as with other living creatures, all kinds of subtleties and mysteries exist in the pike's world. There are still many questions to be answered about its feeding habits.

A good example of this type of question is whether or not the pike has a preferred size of food. In my opinion, the answer is very probably. It is tempting to think of pike as undiscriminating dustbins that patrol the waters looking for anything edible, from as small as minnows to as large as bream. Yet this is probably not the case, for it seems that most pike prefer to eat prey fish of one particular size. It is interesting that again and again pike will take one particular size of bait even though several are offered. In fact, I would go as far as to say that the preferred bait size is roughly 3–6oz. I

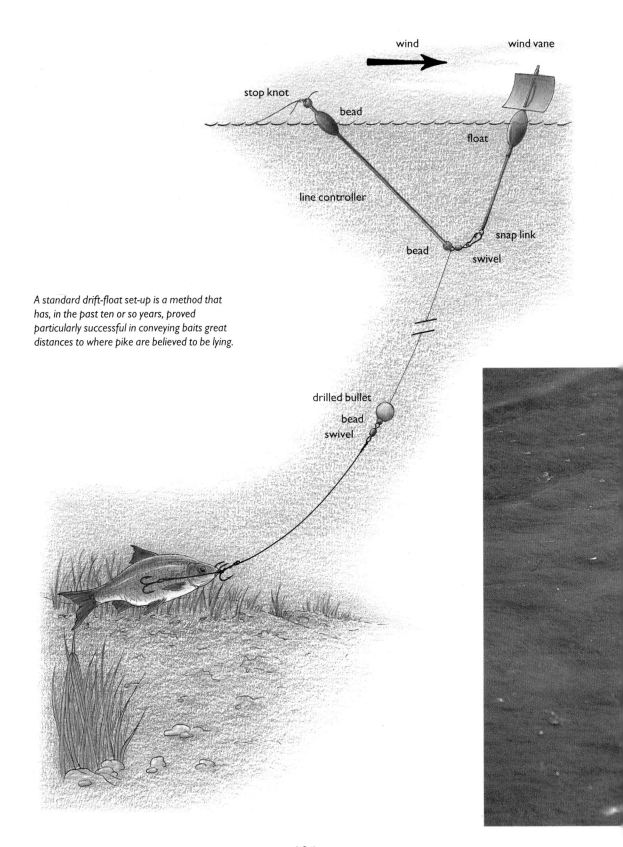

wind

wind vane

stop knot

bead

float

line controller

bead

snap link

swivel

A standard drift-float set-up is a method that
has, in the past ten or so years, proved
particularly successful in conveying baits great
distances to where pike are believed to be lying.

drilled bullet

bead

swivel

accept that on occasion even big pike will eat much smaller fish and at the same time I know that monsters have been caught on live and deadbaits of 2–3lb or even more. But to my mind both extremes are exceptions and I habitually use a bait of around 5–6in for any size of pike. My thinking is simply that, from the pike's point of view, a big bait – and here I mean a livebait – needs a great deal of effort to catch and eat. The following story illustrates this point.

One surprisingly mild December morning I was fishing a deep trough in a large pit where very big pike were known to exist. I was offering a live trout of about 8oz on a float-paternoster rig with a 2oz lead on the bottom. The float began to show signs of the agitation that is often a prelude to an attack on the bait by a pike. The trout appeared on the surface, obviously in distress, and then a very large back appeared behind it. The livebait swam rapidly to the bank, dragging float

This pike is only five yards from the bank but could very easily be missed. A fish of around 8lb, it last fed the previous day on small roach and is now lying in the bottom silt virtually indistinguishable from its surroundings.

and lead behind it. There were swirls as the pike tried to catch the fleeing fish and failed on three occasions. In the end, the frightened trout landed back at my feet and, frustrated as I was, I could not help feeling sorry for the terrified bait and in a way pleased that it had escaped. But sentiment apart, this was a clear example of how a big, lively bait is not an easy proposition even for a pike of 20lb or more.

Equally, I cannot begin to estimate how many hundreds of fair-sized fish – say 1lb or heavier – I have caught with fresh pike wounds on their bodies. Obviously, these sizeable fish have been attacked and perhaps even caught for a short while before struggling free. However, a 4oz roach would find it difficult to flee and then impossible to extricate itself from those jaws once clamped upon it. In nature there are no failsafe rules, but whenever the opportunity presents itself give me a small bait every time.

A dear friend of mine fished a well-known trout lake for pike for seven years without a run! You see, he insisted on using deadbaits. For some reason deadbaits on clear trout waters seem to be next to useless for pike. I emphasize the word 'next' because, of

LOGS WITH EYES

The very first time I tried out my new Kiwi canoe was when I paddled down a reeded, canal-like arm of a lake. As I approached a particular area I was aware of several logs lying half in and half out of the reeds in about two feet of water. Half covered with silt, they had obviously been there for some time. As I was coming back down the canal again, over the logs, I suddenly noticed that one had eyes!

These pike – as the 'logs' turned out to be – were all clustered in a piece of water 40–50 yards long, out of a total length ten times as great. That was interesting in itself and without the Kiwi I would never have found that fact out. However, just as interesting was the fact of the silt that had built up around them: those fish had obviously been lying on the bottom, not moving for several days.

Having found the pike, I investigated repeatedly and it was a further four days before they moved and disappeared off into the lake, almost certainly to feed on a large shoal of roach that had gathered where the canal emptied into the main body of water. They were gone for a day and then returned to their sanctuary in the reeds, where they stayed, again for four days, with the silt building up around them once more.

Although it was only a simple piece of detection, it served to confirm for me that, as others have observed, pike feed, lie comatose for several days while they digest, before bestirring themselves again in response to the pangs of hunger.

This canal-like arm of a large estate lake always holds small fish and the heron, who became quite a friend of mine, knows this as he waits patiently for the ice to thaw. It is here that a large percentage of the lake's pike population chooses to lie low, while they digest their food. Presumably they know they have only a small distance to swim before finding food once hunger stirs again.

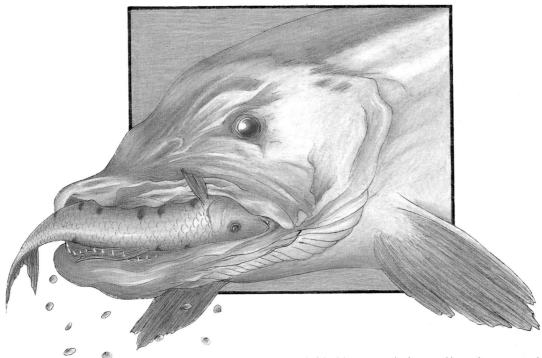

A pike's characteristic way of gripping a roach is to hold it across its mouth. Often showers of scales fall from the distressed prey, and it is possible to walk along clear, shallow rivers and see patches of them lying on the bottom in clearer areas. Almost certainly these indicate pike attacks in the past, but can also point to feeding areas currently used by pike. A bait placed in such an area is much more likely to be taken than one cast out blind without observation or forethought.

course, some pike do fall for deadbaits but very few compared with those that attack livebaits. Why? Surely deadbaits always present an easy meal, and after all they cannot possibly escape. Yet the phenomenon exists – of that there is no doubt. For many years I have fished such waters through the winter and have lost count of the number of trout I have seen that failed to overwinter and lay dead on the bottom, moving very slowly with the underwater currents.

I accept that when the water is very soupy and hunting is a very chancy business then pike will like a good deadbait but it does seem that when it is clear there is something about the thrill of the hunt that is important. The 'thrill of the hunt' – what a careless thing for a detective to say, for surely a pike is just an efficient killing machine, eating to live. Probably so, but not one without brains.

On another occasion I was fishing a very popular pit when bubbles arose around the pike float for the fifth time in two days. The float simply trembled and I

struck. Nothing yet again. I wound in and sure enough there were marks of pike teeth on the bait: nothing much but a pike had obviously been interested. It was a heavily pressured small pike water where most of the fish had been caught at least once or twice. Because the pit was small it did not provide the pike with any real sanctuary areas, yet it allowed me to see exactly – at least at close range – just what was going on. On a very large water it is doubtful whether I would have seen bubbles, a twitching float or any other signs of pike activity. I would have simply have been bemused by those teeth marks, putting them down as one of those things that dog any angler. For the two years that I fished that water I can hardly remember a conventional run: the float might just dip as though a shy roach were taking the bait or 2–3in of line would move out if I were legering. Strikes had to be instant and even then I was very lucky indeed to make contact. The pike might be feeding ravenously, judging by the amount of prey fish clearing the water, but still any take would be cautious and reluctant. Pike are no fools, and you ignore this fact at your peril.

A concealed threat

On the other hand, on heavily fished waters you can easily feel sorry for the pike. It has to eat fish to live and anglers know this and so present them as bait. This means that every single fish presents a possible threat. For a carp this is not the case, and if it does not want to eat boilies, sweetcorn or whatever else happens to be on offer it can simply move back to natural food

THE LESSON OF THE DOLPHIN

Llandegfedd Reservoir is an attractive reservoir of some 400 acres set amid woods and fields in South Wales. Since the late 1980s it has become famous for the abundance of massive pike that have come from its waters, which are most commonly used as a trout fishery. Right from the start, Llandegfedd was a success as a pike fishery, rewriting the record books.

In the early days the fish landed made many experienced anglers gasp but so too did the sight of the 'Dolphin' – massive pike that cavorted fearlessly when things were quiet and the reservoir was comparatively calm. The Dolphin was not the only huge pike to show itself regularly but everybody agreed that it was the biggest. They could never agree on its weight, however, and rumours were rife that it could weigh over 50lb, but it was never caught. However, many rolling pike are feeding fish and can be caught. The odds are that the Dolphin was simply feeding on live rainbow trout or coarse fish, and the rules forbade anything but deadbaits and spinners. Therefore it was the rules rather than nature that left the Dolphin uncaptured and unweighed.

To my mind there is little doubt that pike that roll on the surface like the Dolphin are in fact feeding, often quite hard if you can find exactly the right bait, nearly always a live one,

This very large Scottish pike water lies unnaturally still at dawn. Very soon after this shot was taken, two pike began to roll ten yards or so from the bank. At first it was hard to see any reason for this but then a shoal of char appeared in the same area, dimpling the surface for insects. What I am sure was happening was that the char had attracted the pike in, triggering off feeding, and the surface indications were proof of this.

Roger Miller is about to net a big Scottish pike. It was just one of a number that he caught from a large bay in a week's fishing during May. He located the bay purely through eyesight, seeing surface movement one evening when the water was calm. His original estimation was that about ten pike might be in the bay but happily the catches proved that there were far more.

and can swim it out towards the pike and let it work in the general area. Quite why pike break surface in this peculiar slow, heavy motion remains a mystery.

On Llandegfedd, most of the boats head towards the north bank, where they fish an area of relatively shallow water, and into Sor Bay, where there are often great concentrations of roach and dace. On a large water like this it pays to scan the water, looking for surface movements that betray the presence of fish. Llandegfedd is fished from boats but it could well be that here and on other waters craft disturb pike, especially in calm conditions and it would be better to make a long cast in these circumstances. Of course, if there is anything like a ripple at all then the drifter-float method can be used to move the bait into the desired area. The successful angler will be the one who keeps his eyes open and his wits about him.

items. The pike cannot: it must eat fish and every one it takes could have hooks in it.

Imagine this scene: huge shoals of roach lift from the water on a calm morning a little after light has broken, and pike, singly or in a group, are striking into them, on the prowl, attacking in an open, positive fashion. Somewhere, several feet below the surface an eel swims out from between two stones where it has been resting. It moves a few feet and is engulfed. A pike knew exactly where the eel was lying and had mounted an ambush, simply waiting for the moment when the prey should decide to leave. Two modes of attack,

both successful and each demanding different skills on the part of the pike; skills inherited to ensure the future of the individual fish and the species. It is vital that any pike angler recognizes these two modes of attack and plans his own pursuit accordingly.

Therefore, when pike are feeding in a rampant fashion, careering into shoals of prey fish, it makes sense to use a livebait if possible, a roaming livebait fished under a light float, unhindered by leads, and paid out on a floating line. The efforts of the prey fish and any wind influence will ensure that the bait moves here and there, working and searching the water for

A pike attacks a shoal of fish, simply lunging and seizing those that are closest and easiest to pick off.

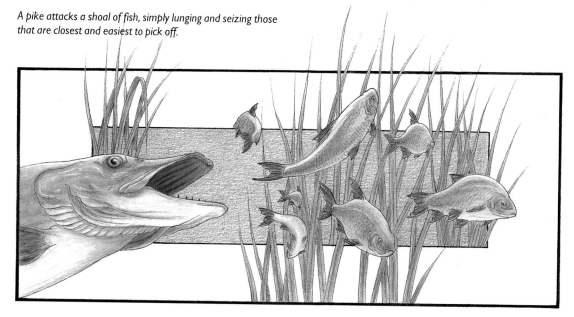

Left: This is only a small pike but see how magnificent its markings are and how well it blends in with the background. There are two plausible reasons for this. First, it needs its camouflage to protect it from predators such as herons or large pike. Second, it is learning to hunt for itself and needs to be able to ambush small roach, bleak and other fry if it is to survive through the winter.

Right: Pike take a considerable time to digest a meal, and indeed if they have fed well they might lie up for three days or more. During this time they are in a near-comatose state and silt may well build up on them, disguising them to some extent. It is as though they were dead to the world, but as soon as hunger strikes again they shake off their temporary camouflage of debris and begin to stalk prey once more.

the pike that you know are on the feed. In most cases you will not have long to wait before the livebait swims itself to its own fate.

A lot of pike, bigger ones often, are the ambush-feeding type and with them you need to adopt a different, more patient approach. The detective will know the sort of places where a big pike tends to lurk: generally somewhere around snags, along drop-offs, around old pit machinery or wherever there is a chance of blending into the background in an area that prey fish often frequent. A deadbait is easy to fish in these places but a livebait should be tethered on either a floating or a sunken paternoster. Sometimes you will need to leave the bait out for an hour or even much longer, until the pike either appears or grows hungry enough to sidle in and attack.

It might not look particularly exciting but this photograph records one of the most thrilling moments of an angler's life. The scene is Llandegfedd Reservoir. One of the boats has just had success and, following tradition, motors in to the north bank, where the fish is unhooked and weighed. The Ranger's boat (the bigger boat) also comes in to supervise. In this case, the fish being weighed was a fraction over 30lb.

An early September morning and a shoal of roach are penned
in the deeper water down by the dam by several pike that
take it in turns to hunt. Here are several hundred roach
churning up the water as a pike of 12lb powers into them.
Predators like this are very susceptible to a small livebait
which, working under a float on a greased line, can cover a
fair amount of water.

HANDLING PIKE

A tragedy of angling is the history of good pike waters that have been all but wiped out by bad, careless or clueless handling of the fish. The fact is that although many anglers set out to catch pike a great number of them are absolutely terrified of their quarry when it is on the bank. There is something about the close-set eyes, the leering mouth and the sharp teeth that is guaranteed to cloud reason, judgement and, vitally, unhooking skills. This is why so many big pike have been left with hooks inside them or have been pulled and prodded at until the gills have begun to bleed and they have died alone, back in the water, and rotted there. If we are to continue catching pike then we must preserve them and the best way to do that is to unhook them quickly, cleanly and safely.

The best way to unhook a pike cleanly begins long before it is even landed! Firstly, you must have good sensitive bite indication so that you can tell at once that a pike has picked up the bait. Good drop-back indicators, buzzers or a sensitive float set-up are what are needed and – equally important – you must be there watching and listening all the time.

Striking at the right time

Next make sure that your hooks are barbless or at least only semi-barbed. This can make a tremendous difference when it comes to taking out a deeply set hook. Finally, always strike quickly, within seconds of the bite developing. If you do strike early and lose a fish it does not matter, for the chances are that it is a small pike anyway. If the pike is of a decent size the earliest strike will almost inevitably secure a hookhold at the front of the mouth, where unhooking is much easier.

When you have the pike there in your net, ready to put on the bank, be careful that it does not spin round and the hook get caught up in the mesh, making the task that faces you even harder. Take the pike from the

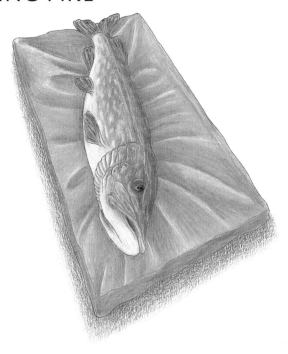

As soon as a pike is landed it should be laid on a soft surface, preferably a purpose-made rubber unhooking mat. This protects the pike, and other species, from unnecessary harm and is a worthwhile investment. Always wet the unhooking mat before laying a fish on it.

net and lay it for preference on an unhooking mat or, at worst, on deep, damp grass. Hold the fish firmly and confidently, for it will only squirm and fall, and in no circumstances lift it far above the ground.

Once the pike is on the mat turn it onto its back and if necessary straddle it with your leg so that it cannot wander. You will now find that if you insert your hand under its bottom jaw the mouth will open automatically and allow you free access into the cavernous

Taken on a large reservoir-type lure, this pike was hooked cleanly on the outside of the mouth, as virtually all fly-caught pike are. I am sure fly fishing for pike, which is already practised widely in North America, will begin to catch on in Britain in the coming years. It is clean, efficient and exciting and without a doubt poses far less threat to the pike's safety than a livebait or a deadbait.

Right: Many novices unhook pike extremely clumsily and as a result not only get cut by their needle-like teeth but also cause the pike to suffer. Efficient unhooking depends on a combination of the right tools, the ability to use them safely, and confidence, for it is no use going about the task half-heartedly. If the hooks are set deep you can often get at them through the gill flap. Grasp the shank of the hook with the forceps and gently twist to release the barbs, although nowadays barbless hooks are rightly regarded as a better choice. This operation is made much easier if a companion pulls on the wire trace to keep it taut. If you place the fish on its back and straddle it with your knees you will find that it remains quite docile and does not wriggle, and so harms neither you nor itself.

Below: If you choose to weigh the fish, do it quickly in a ready-made weighing sack, wetted beforehand. The scales should be zeroed and ready so that the operation is over in a few seconds and trauma to the fish is minimized.

mouth. By now the fish will be still, its mouth will be open and you will be in complete control. For your own peace of mind, wear gloves, but you will probably not need them now and you can get to work with one or two pairs of forceps and even operate on quite a deeply hooked fish (which should be a rarity if you obey the rules above). With practice you will soon be able to return pike as unmarked as when you caught them, and have the satisfaction of knowing that you have done no harm whatsoever. Big pike deserve respect and there is no reason why yours should not go back completely unharmed.

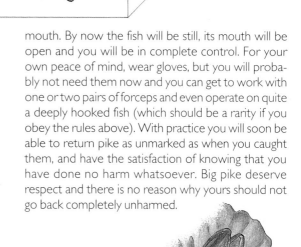

Right: If the pike is to be photographed, hold it carefully and confidently. The diagram shows how the hands should be positioned to ensure maximum security and an impressive picture.

AN UNKNOWN LAKE

Every so often an angler's dream is answered – an invitation arrives to fish an unknown lake. One such water that I was lucky enough to fish covers about two acres, is quite old and is sheltered on three sides by very mature trees, with the northern side open to pasture fields. The water was constructed around the turn of the century by damming the small stream and certainly the bottom end is much the deeper. A great deal of silting has gone on at the top and what was obviously once an island is now actually part of the bank.

Promising signs

My first visit was in early July when the water was tinged brown and visibility was about two feet. I immediately liked the place. The beds of arrowhead-lilies made everything particularly attractive, and I suspected that they might harbour predators of some kind. I also liked the look of a bulrush clump on the left-hand bank as I looked up the lake, for in my experience bulrushes, hard lake beds and tench have usually gone together. But as I did not have a clue what was in the lake I set up normal float gear and two maggots on a size 14 hook.

Soon on every cast I was landing small roach of 3–6oz – in short, nothing very special at all despite shifting depths and increasing the number of maggots to three or even four. I had half-hoped for a tench or perhaps even a small carp but it was roach after roach in the growing sunshine.

A flexible approach

Around 10 o'clock I noticed that the roach action had begun to slow down and I wondered if I had actually begun to scare the shoal or even to thin it out. Then, as I was reeling in another roach, it was grabbed momentarily and the rod hooped over before springing back straight. The roach had gone. Shortly after, a few roach scattered just out of the swim and one was actually chased three or four yards along the surface, followed by quite a large bow-wave. Obviously predators were at work and I set up a second rod. This was simply slightly heavier gear, with a larger float carrying two large shot and a size 4 single hook. I used a short wire trace to attach the hook to the line since I reckoned that pike were probably the culprits. For bait, I killed the next roach, cut it in half and mounted the tailpiece on the hook.

In the next hour and a half I had three very promising runs on pieces of roach which I missed. The fourth run, however, I struck into and soon landed a pike of around 5lb. This might appear to have solved the mystery but I was not totally satisfied that those first three

Perch waters do not have to be large to produce very big perch. In fact, provided the foodstocks exist, big perch can even thrive in a goldfish pond, and I have seen a four-pounder taken from one only three yards long. Having been feeding there on very small goldfish for some two years, it had grown to this remarkable size. So, even though this lake covers only about two acres, it holds a lot of small roach and this is the key. In addition, the water is clear, with visibility of at least 4ft – a vital element in any big-perch water.

One of the reasons that makes this one of the most prolific perch waters in the West Country and Wales is the mass of lilies, for these provide adult perch with an excellent spawning ground and the perchlings with an abundance of safe refuge.

runs were actually from pike. For one thing, the bait had come back to me each time and had no visible teeth marks puncturing it. However, each time a few scales had actually been scuffed away from the skin – very unpike-like behaviour. Also, the pike that I landed was very well hooked and I could not understand why the first three runs had been missed if pike, too, had been responsible. But time had run out, as I had to go somewhere else that day. Rather baffled and not a little frustrated, I packed up, looking forward eagerly to the next trip, for by now I had my suspicions.

A few days later I was back. Four runs produced nothing but pike. And so the story went on several more trips. I might easily have put the first session down to eels, perhaps, unexpectedly active in the daylight that first July morning. However, in October, a

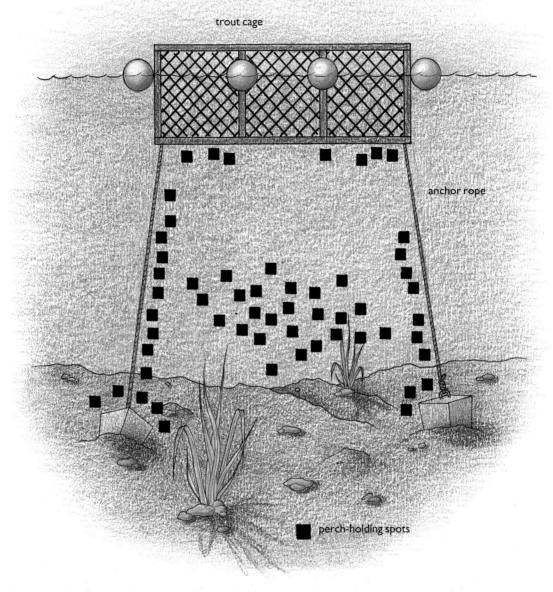

trout cage

anchor rope

■ perch-holding spots

friend rang up, quite jubilant, to say that he had just caught a perch of 3lb 2oz from the lake.

After offering my congratulations I sat down to try and analyse the capture. My feeling was and is that my friend's perch was the only, or at least almost the only, example of the species in that water. Perhaps it represented all that remained of a previous perch population that had dwindled drastically. Certainly, there appear to be no small perch in the water at all and the stock will inevitably die out altogether if it has not already. My suspicion that what I had encountered was not a pike was right, but I only wish I had known that little lake before the total demise of its perch.

Above and above right: It is useful to know that perch tend to gather in shoals wherever there is an obstruction in the water. A good example is a trout cage, and they will frequent the water directly underneath it or linger near the ropes securing it. A boat is another favoured obstruction, perch often moving under it within an hour of its being moored.

Right: This photograph reveals more than a pretty perch with an aggressive dorsal fin. The clue is the background. Perch and rocks go together almost invariably, and indeed the ingredients that make a big-perch water are clarity, lilies or Canadian pondweed and plenty of rocks on the bottom. Provided small fish are present in quantity, big perch almost always thrive in such habitats.

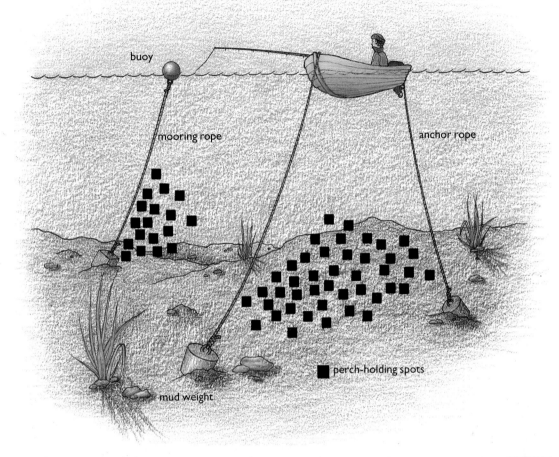

buoy

mooring rope

anchor rope

perch-holding spots

mud weight

WEED CAMOUFLAGE

For all my fishing life I have been aware that perch and waters which have Canadian pondweed go together frequently if not almost always – unless disaster has occurred. But never did I consciously try to understand the connection between the two until a recent piece of investigative work on a canal in France. The day was very hot, and although the water looked scummy and uninviting, it seemed to be worth calling a brief halt. As soon as I looked into the murk and saw Canadian pondweed I began to think perch – and I was to be proved right.

A large shoal of tiny catfish about 1in long came into view, dancing and weaving the most intricate of patterns. They approached a bank of weed and almost immediately a couple of

strands broke away, or so it seemed, and plunged into the shimmering shoal of baby cats. In fact, these fronds of pondweed were small perch of about 2–3oz, but to my eye, from above, they had been totally indistinguishable from the plant itself.

Naturally, everything looks different from under the surface, but the viewpoint of predatory water birds – for example, the heron – cannot differ greatly from ours. It seems likely then that the camouflage offered by profuse Canadian pondweed gives young perch a reasonable chance to establish themselves through those critical first months or season or two before they are big enough and wily enough to fend for themselves.

This photograph was taken in central France and the tadpole-like creatures are tiny catfish, probably around two hundred in number and forming a tight, wriggling ball. A couple of feet away, and hidden under stones in the bank, perch repeatedly darted out to attack.

Perch are often very vulnerable to a small spinner, as this one proved. What I did not expect to see was such extraordinary coloration.

A DOUBLE ATTACK

It was a very still October morning in 1987, under a sky that was cloudless after a touch of frost the night before. Surprisingly, given the high atmospheric pressure, a clear water and the bright morning sunshine, fish were feeding busily – predators that is. I choose this memory with good reason, for at that time both pike and perch were present in the lake in good numbers and the evidence was there to see.

Pike or perch?

Between 7.00 and 9.30am a large roach shoal lifted from the water six times. I estimated that about five or six hundred fish of 4–6in long made up this shoal and they covered an area of a good-sized room. Sometimes, in the centre of the disturbance, there would be a large boil or splash. In my experience, this method of attack is absolutely typical of pike, probably acting singly but sometimes, perhaps, in small groups.

Ten times, another shoal of roach, slightly smaller,

A perch attacks in a slightly different way from a pike, targeting a particular fish rather than simply the easiest, and then chasing it until it is caught or escapes. This is often what is happening when you see small fish skittering several yards along the surface, pursued by a bow-wave, and sometimes a section of the predator's spiked dorsal fin. The perch harries the prey, nipping at its tail in an attempt to foil its escape.

that was wandering around a reed fringe, showered out in similar fashion. But then there was a secondary attack. By that I mean single, small fish could be seen fleeing from the primary attack area, pursued, chillingly, by large bow-waves. Repeatedly four or five of these waves would leave the primary attack area, indicating that a shoal of predatory fish – clearly perch – were at work. Very often the prey fish left the water in five or six mini-leaps before the whole spectacle would end in medium-sized swirls. It was obvious what was happening: the shoals of good perch – their average size was 2½lb – were cornering a roach shoal against the reedbeds and attacking upwards into them. Any perch that had not made a kill in this initial attack would then single out a roachling to pursue. This pursuit almost always follows a classic fashion: the perch harries and chases, slashing at the end of the fish until it is sufficiently immobilized to be caught. Sometimes this can take ten yards to effect and sometimes the roach even manages to make its escape.

Four times that morning there were four primary attacks only and in the mayhem I could clearly see the dorsal fins of the perch. The fact that there were no secondary attacks signifies to me that kills were made in the initial charge.

I emphasize that what I saw that morning was very typical, classic hunting behaviour on the part of both

pike and perch and that their different attack modes could very easily be differentiated. However, there are times when the distinction is not so clear. For example, in rough, windy weather or at distance it is more difficult to make an exact identification. Also, if there are only one or two attacks then you have to watch very closely indeed to make any type of decision.

Does all this matter? If you see the signs of predatorial activity, why not just put out a small live or dead-bait and wait to see the result? Well, perhaps most vitally, many big perch will not take a bait on a wire trace – they are simply too wary to do that. Now, that means that if you have to use a bait on nylon and the culprit is a pike, then you are very likely to suffer bite-offs and leave a fish with a hook in its mouth – which we should never risk. So, if you are sure that perch are the culprits you can fish for them with nylon with hope and a clear conscience.

Above: In the foreground you see the rings of small fish dibbling on the surface but behind them comes a menacing bow-wave. This was made by a 2¼lb perch entering the shoal, looking for its breakfast. It succumbed to a small livebait presented under a tiny float.

Left: A good perch comes to the net with the tail of the livebait still quite visible in its mouth. Perch nearly always swallow the head first, so it is best to put the hooks around that area.

BLINKERED BY BARBEL

In the summer of 1991 I was fishing a big, deep hole below a bridge that was positively heaving with barbel. Barbel. Barbel and more barbel. Barbel were all I could think of or want to catch. They filled my every waking hour and every dreaming minute.

One strange thing, though: for over two days, virtually every time the feeder went into the water there would first be frenzied fish activity only to be followed soon afterwards by a heavy splashing. Yet so forthcoming were the barbel bites that I never really gave this strange surface disturbance any thought.

Then, on the third day I lost the swim. A nightbird had beaten me to it, and there he was, hunched over his rod in the grey dawn. I wandered off upriver and returned mid-morning – without barbel this time – just to see how he had fared. He had hooked and returned three perch, all unweighed but the largest was 18in – a three-pounder for sure!

I just could not believe it! But then, if I had not been so blind I would have seen that everything fitted in. I had been mixing the groundbait in the feeder quite dry, so some had obviously come out on impact with the river. After a while, the bleak, the dace and the minnows had come to recognize that the splash meant showering titbits for them. Soon after that, those big perch had realized that a splash meant a congregation of unaware little fish. What a fool I had been! I had even taken a quick photograph of the phenomenon, so much had it interested me. So why on earth had I not gone that step further and actually investigated with a tiny deadbait? Need I add that the next day, my feeder went in with all the usual frenzied activity but no splashing followed. The shoal of perch had simply moved on and never again did I find them there. Fishing detective! My utter blindness to the real situation had probably cost me some of the biggest perch I had ever come near to catching.

An explosion of small fish, forced to the surface by feeding perch. This was one situation where I should not have been content just to take a photograph but should have investigated further.

EXTRAORDINARY DETECTION

Perch are fascinating creatures and it is no wonder that there is a large and thriving club dedicated to their pursuit. But the fact remains that they are often more difficult to locate than catch. I remember hearing the well-known Norfolk angler John Nunn talk about his experiences on a large reservoir with fish-locating equipment to help him. Certainly, that day, the screen displayed something quite out of the ordinary. John tells the story in his own words:

'With a fish locator at my disposal for the day, I rode out on the reservoir, excited by its considerable reputation for large perch. As you might expect in winter, vast areas of water proved to be devoid of fish: frequently areas that looked right and had attractive

A large water in a foggy December dawn. It is at times like this that locating perch can be quite a problem and any clues are gratefully seized on. You will notice here a large congregation of waterfowl, which, I am convinced, play a role rather like the boats and mooring ropes in John Nunn's story. Provided they stay in one general area long enough, they will attract perch to them in great numbers.

depth variation were places where it would have been easy to waste long periods of a short winter day.

'First indications of fish were seen in thirty feet of water, where a number of snags showed up on the reservoir bed, presumably tree stumps. As I progressed along the reservoir arm, correlation between submerged trees and shoals of fish became more distinct. I fished alongside the stumps, taking perch from each area that were shown to have a congregation of fish. The reservoir is used by a sailing club for racing. They mark their racing courses with permanently moored buoys. These buoys and their ropes form the only features in an otherwise featureless area. Hundreds of yards of empty water, then a single rope and around that rope a congregation of fish. After fishing around these mooring ropes and catching large numbers of perch to around a pound, I decided that an experiment was needed.

A focus of interest

'I rode over to an area of the reservoir which the locator screen showed as having no fish in it – a difficult thing to force myself into doing, but it was in the interests of scientific research after all. The nearest concentration of fish was around one of the trout cages some fifty yards away. I lowered the boat's mooring weights to the bottom, some thirty-two feet below me. After fifty minutes the fish locator showed the

arrival of a few fish close to the bottom. Sure enough, bites started to come and fish came regularly to the net. Sport became hectic and a glance at the screen showed why – a large shoal had collected underneath the boat, seemingly attracted by the mooring ropes and weights. I had created a feature for them to home-in on.

'I rode back reflecting on the reasons behind the pattern that the fish locator uncovered. I am tempted to say never mind the reasons – at least if we know what does happen, we can make the most of that knowledge. Nevertheless, the thinking angler should be asking questions. Perhaps the perch find something to eat on the ropes? But as the boat's mooring ropes spend half their time out of the water, what possible nutrition can be found on their man-made fibres? I would expect the mooring ropes of the trout pens and sailing-club buoys to be more attractive. The perch may graze them in the same way sea fish may be observed grazing mooring ropes in a harbour.

'I am not keen on the suggestion that the boat acts as an attraction. What difference could it make to life thirty-feet below? I purposely did not put any maggots or worms around the boat to attract fish, so that the experiment could not be influenced by such an obvious man-made attraction. I have spoken to others who have fished the reservoir and they have all commented, without any prompting from me, that as their

Left: A perfect perch water – rocks, great clarity and splendid weed growth. Waters like this are best explored with small live fish rather than deadbaits.

Right: It is quite a sight to watch perch rubbing themselves on underwater features such as piers or tree roots. They plainly enjoy vigorous physical contact, and in this way provide an important clue to the fishing detective. A bait fished hard up against a submerged obstruction, man-made or natural, is likely to be taken swiftly and very voraciously.

day progressed they caught more fish in the area immediately next to the boat. So, the ropes would seem to be the attracting feature. At least you can set out confident that casting is unlikely to be important – just lower your bait over the side!'

What John has to say is fascinating. In particular I like the theory that the perch may graze on the mooring ropes for some food items. I have often seen perch in the area of rocks and underwater snags and moorings. Perhaps they were doing the same there and filtering

Above: I spent an instructive half an hour watching this perch of about 1 ½lb grazing around rocks, hunting for small fish. During that time it scared out at least twenty minnows, managing to catch three of them.

off food too small to use on a hook. However, I remember one particular estate lake in the summer of 1989. I was on a landing-stage and my attention was caught by two big perch, at my feet, twisting round and round the legs of the wooden structure. I watched

them for several minutes and there was no doubt that they were rubbing themselves against the pilings like a cat does against your legs. Possibly that is the attraction of the ropes to perch, and maybe anything that provides a scratching post in the water will draw them.

I am not totally convinced, however, that we ought to completely write off the importance of changes in light. On several rivers the very best perch swims are below overhanging trees where obviously the light enters the water in a diluted and broken stream. In lakes, too, dense reedbeds frequently prove the most attractive places for perch shoals. Is this because the light is constantly reflected and refracted or because they like to rub their bodies against the stems or because there is food for them to graze upon there? Perhaps the answer is a combination of all three factors. Whatever the truth, there is certainly detective work still to be done before this puzzle is solved.

Below: Changes in the light are very important to perch and their bodies are very prone to picking up underwater shafts of light that could prove potentially fatal if a big predator is in the area. To take a graphic example, this picture shows a group of perch in a deep river pocket, and every now and then one of these half-pounders twists to catch an item of food. Every time it does so its body shows up quite clearly. As there were no overhanging trees or anything to dilute the strength of the sunlight, the fish were very vulnerable.

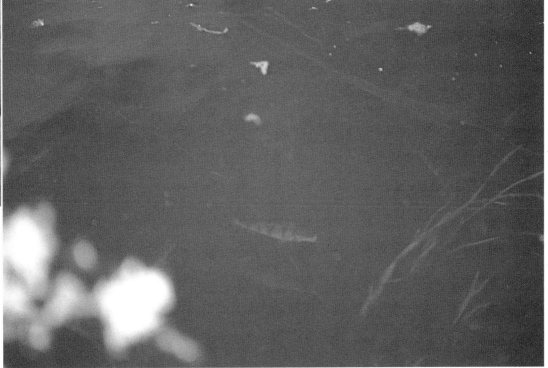

FRY FEEDING

Especially during the autumn, the fry of the spring spawning tend to remain in huge shoals, waiting for the winter. By now a lot of the fish are 1in or more in length, and so a viable food form for even large predators, provided they can be taken in numbers.

It is at times like this that pike tend to shoal together and hunt the fry masses. In an exciting, savage process that can last for hours, vast carpets of fry lift over and over as the pike plough into them with their mouths open, swallowing the titbits like whales gorge on plankton. At times perch do the same thing, swimming high in the water, dorsals outstretched, as they take two or three small fish before turning down again to chew and to swallow.

Fry feeding can cause the angler an enormous headache: the pike become preoccupied with the small fish and so only the smallest livebait will work any magic at all. Consider the problems of mounting a 1in bait on a suitable hook. Sometimes, two small fish

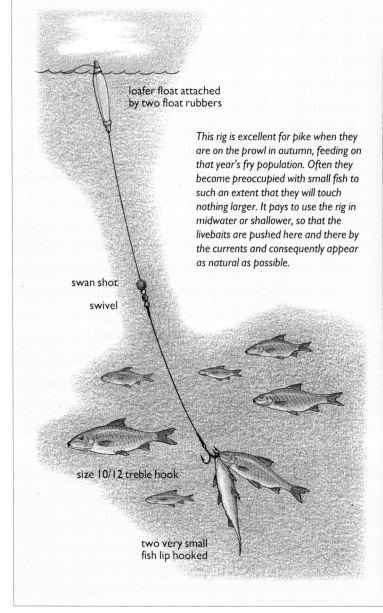

loafer float attached
by two float rubbers

This rig is excellent for pike when they are on the prowl in autumn, feeding on that year's fry population. Often they become preoccupied with small fish to such an extent that they will touch nothing larger. It pays to use the rig in midwater or shallower, so that the livebaits are pushed here and there by the currents and consequently appear as natural as possible.

swan shot

swivel

size 10/12 treble hook

two very small
fish lip hooked

on each point of a treble hook will work and occasionally pike will look at a slightly bigger bait than the fry, say a gudgeon of 2–3in, which can be fished quite effectively. There are times too when a small spinner or plug drawn quite quickly up near the surface will be taken.

Fry feeding is an absorbing sight as well as a real challenge. For both reasons it pays to take binoculars on larger waters and constantly scan the bays and reedy margins where the prey fish often attempt to congregate.

In these late-summer shallows the chub and roach fry of the spring have grown to around about 1in. Their favourite haunt is along very shallow gravels where cattle come to drink. The perch know this, and shoals of them hang in slightly deeper water, sweeping in throughout the day to harass the small fish and pick up what they can. Here some perch of nearly 1½lb are pushing the fry almost onto the bank itself. A very small deadbait cast out into the current and allowed to trundle downstream produced instant results, taking a fish of just over 1¼lb.

THE CAT'S WHISKERS

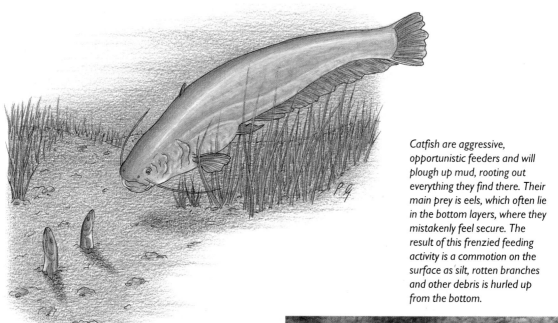

Catfish are aggressive, opportunistic feeders and will plough up mud, rooting out everything they find there. Their main prey is eels, which often lie in the bottom layers, where they mistakenly feel secure. The result of this frenzied feeding activity is a commotion on the surface as silt, rotten branches and other debris is hurled up from the bottom.

Catfish, and angling for them, are on the increase in Britain, and what I describe below could soon be, if not common, at least a spectacle to be witnessed occasionally in this country. In addition, the story illustrates a graphic example of detection.

It was August and I was standing by a large lake in central France. The rain was bucketing down and I took shelter under a vast oak tree along with a local pole angler. We talked for a while about fishing matters, here, there and the world over. He showed me his sophisticated tackle and bait, as well as the net of roach he had taken, which he would soon take home to eat! And when he pulled out a bottle of red wine from his sack, the afternoon took on a positively encouraging glow. Somewhere into our second glass, something appalling took place out in the dark water.

About 50 yards from us a vast area, at least 30 feet long and half as wide, became convulsed with bubbles and rising silt, branches, rubbish and the scum of years past. It was really like an underwater volcano – so violent that you could actually smell the lake bed erupting in the wet air. The tumultuous activity continued for a minute and then slowly died away. We both watched, without exchanging a word. I felt distinctly frightened in that strange, gloomy place. 'What on earth was that?' I asked when it was quiet again. My French friend shrugged: 'It is nothing! Just an old catfish,' he replied, holding his arms as wide as they could possibly stretch.

'About that big. Two metres long perhaps. What they do is dive into the bottom to unearth the eels. They spin round and eat them.' He made a snapping motion with his mouth. 'Look, they're gone.' He made a wriggling motion with his fingers. 'All those little eels gone, down into the depths!' he said with a hearty laugh.

Perhaps he was right. A little while later I was fishing in some marshes around the Caspian Sea and several times saw smaller eruptions very similar to the one that I had witnessed in France. Each time catfish were caught very shortly afterwards. It certainly makes sense, the idea of a big bottom feeder diving into the silt to unearth food that would be dopey and very easy for cats to catch.

This story shows that often, right before our eyes, fish give us unmistakable clues to their behaviour. Despite this, in Britain catfish seem to have built up a reputation as avowed bottom feeders, scavengers, their long feelers probing for food in the mud or on the silt. Again around the Caspian Sea, I fished for them in a crystal-clear network of lagoons and what I saw there seemed to give the lie to, or at least modify, this image of a lethargic, sinister hunter.

In clear water it was quite possible to see the catfish hunting actively in mid-water or even near the surface. The preferred method of the locals was to spin for them with very small (nos. 2 and 3) Mepps. The catfish sensed these with their feelers and homed in incredibly quickly for a kill. It was obvious that their feelers did a great deal of work because from time to time they were actually momentarily foul-hooked before the trebles broke away from such a slender hold. And these were big fish: one estimated at 75lb actually slashed at the nets right on the surface in a huge boil but missed.

Perhaps in this country, too, we ought to readjust our thinking and see catfish more as active, high-profile hunters and not simply grubbers along the bottom!

I leave you to make up your own mind about this shot. You might be able to see things in the background that give you an idea of the scale of the underwater eruption. Even now, all I know is that whatever caused it must have possessed immense power.

DETECTION IN RIVERS

VIEW FROM A BRIDGE

When I think of rivers I almost invariably think of their bridges and the exciting and instructive days that I have spent scrambling around on the bridges themselves, on the shadowy banks beneath them and even on the footings of their pillars. Indeed bridges have always had a magnetic appeal for any angler willing to use his eyes, and the reasons are obvious to the fishing detective. In short, many years of observation of the link between bridges and good fishing convince me that no serious angler can afford to pass one without, at the very least, stopping to gaze intently over the parapet.

Vitally, the height of even a low bridge offers a perfect vantage point. A bridge is much like any overhanging tree except that it is much easier to climb onto and offers you a much wider area of water to scan. It is a great advantage to be able to look down virtually vertically onto a river's features and fish-holding swims in particular. No method of observation can beat it, not even swimming in the water among the fish, which can pay dividends but is obviously more disruptive.

For many hundreds of years bridges have been a major, integral part of river systems. They are perfect examples of the way we mould the forces of nature in that most tend to create an area of slower, deeper and more stable water above them. The river simply slows down as it meets the pillars of the bridge and is held up

The parapet of a large, eighteenth-century bridge overlooking the River Wye. It not only offered a fine view but also turned out to be a splendid vantage point for some subsequent angling adventures.

to some extent by them. Below the bridge the situation is quite different and the river funnels through between the arches to gush out into bridge pools numbering from one to as many as a dozen on the widest of rivers.

It is the bridge pool itself that generally causes the greatest excitement in anglers. Historically, bridge pools have produced the most impressive fish and the most dramatic fishing, and the reasons are not hard to find. First, the pillars squeeze the river so that it gushes out with renewed energy and force. Over the years this tends to gouge out the river bed, creating a pool much deeper than the surrounding water. The depth of this pool is of great importance, for it provides both a degree of shelter from the current and shade from bright light.

The attraction of currents

The very existence of a bridge pool, with its haven of deeper water, would in itself be quite enough to attract fish, but there is more. These pools generally have several different currents operating within them, for quicker water flows through the centre of the pool and then slower water works its way back, eddying round the sides. There are also areas of totally slack water behind the pillars themselves. All these areas attract in particular barbel, chub, roach and perch, depending on the time of the day, the season and the condition of the water.

Also, bridge pools are generally rich in obstructions, and in many cases these take the form of stones

CHUB AND HAIR-RIGS

Difficult chub – and what chub are not difficult much of their lives? – have always interested me. So, when hair-rigs first hit the scene many years ago, and soon established a reputation for their effectiveness with carp, I felt that here was a possible answer to all my problems. Accordingly, I learnt all I could about hair-rigs, and went down to the river and tried them out with great enthusiasm. There was no doubt that the chub accept a bait on a hair with considerable alacrity, but putting the hook itself in their mouths proved virtually impossible.

From everything that I observed, it appeared that chub do not feed like carp or even barbel. Instead of toying with and perhaps mouthing the bait where it is presented, they tend to pick it up between their lips, run off with it and then swallow it a little later on. This means that they pick up the bait without taking in the hook and then feel the resistance of the lead and spit the whole lot out. Or the hair, which is of necessity thin and therefore vulnerable, actually breaks.

Now, I have heard that some people have made the hair-rig work with chub, but I have never been able to. It seems that way with bream too – another species that refuses to suck the bait in in a cooperative fashion. There would be so many advantages if bream and chub played the game. But, at least as far as this particular detective can tell, they resolutely refuse to.

A close-up of a very large roach. Specimen roach are inevitably shy-biting and present a considerable challenge. Therefore some of the reasons that make the hair-rig so productive with carp suggest that it should work with big roach too. And yet for some reason, roach have rarely been fished for with a hair-rig, so here is an interesting piece of detective work waiting to be tried out.

Here you can see the strength of a powerful river, its water funnelled through a bridge and out into the waiting pool. For ten yards the force of the water has gouged out a deep channel that is home to bream, roach and some large pike.

or bricks that are a relic from a long-defunct bridge. With all its crooks and crevices that harbour all manner of insect life, partly or fully submerged masonry is highly attractive to fish. Sometimes the bricks on even a new bridge work loose and are prised off by youngsters and tossed into the pool to add to the confusion down there. As the police are well aware, the depths of bridge pools are also one of the favourite dumping grounds for thieves anxious to get rid of useless swag. In this way, electrical equipment, machinery and even office ledgers and books all provide snaggy sanctuary for fish over the years. You would be also surprised how many old prams, bikes and even cars find their way into bridge pools – dumped by thoughtless owners who have no further use for them. Again, the underwater architecture grows – to the benefit of both fish and angler.

There is yet another reason why bridge pools act as a magnet to fish. Consider the number of pedestrians who cross over most bridges in a day, many of them pausing to look for a minute and perhaps even to toss in a bit of food to see if fish can be raised or water birds will congregate. This haphazard diet of bread, biscuits, cake and potato crisps might not amount to a great deal but it is a small and interesting top-up for the fish population below.

This concentration on the downstream water does not mean, however, that we should ignore the stretch of river above the bridge. Many species, especially barbel, use the bridge pool as a daytime haunt but then, at dusk, through the night and well into the early morning, fan out and feed extensively both above and below the bridge pool. Indeed, at first light, on any barbel river, a very common sight is shoals of barbel moving steadily over the gravels away from the pool itself. They can easily be spotted either by the flash of their sides as they turn or by the puffs of silt that are thrown up as they burrow in the gravel for caddis in particular.

WISING UP

I remember once, many years ago when I was far from being a fishing detective, saying that if you could see a chub then you could catch it. How often that glib and stupid statement has come back to haunt me! In fact, I now readily accept that chub are just about the cleverest of coarse fish. It is also interesting that so many big-fish men seem not to like chub and curse them when they come along instead of the expected roach or barbel. Chub deserve our respect and are far more than a substitute for something better.

A merry dance

Ironically, nowadays it is the intelligence of chub that really attracts me, and as an exercise in using detection to second-guess the quarry the story of 'Moby Dick' is worth recounting. I first saw him one July in a well-worn swim above Norwich that is known to all who fish thereabouts. At first I took him for a small to medium-sized common carp, so great was his width and so large were his scales. Only when he turned and surged up through the water did I see him for what he was – an immensely long, deep and broad chub. I have always wanted a six-pounder and now here was one saying hello to me. Apart from his size, the only strangeness about the fish was an ivory whiteness to his head and his left flank. I named him Moby Dick on account of both his hugeness and his colour. And just as that famous whale led Captain Ahab a merry dance

over the seven seas, so was that chub to taunt me on the Wensum.

I soon learned that the fish was a hungry one but that two problems stood in my way. First, he was one of a shoal of thirty lesser specimens. Second, he was clever, a mastermind of the underwater world. I came to learn that if ever a fish should prove capable of thought on a near-human level then Moby would be a good candidate for that distinction.

A great number of Moby's companions, each as hungry as chub always seem to be, convinced me that it was hopeless to fish blind or at night. Over three days a dozen chub to 4lb proved that I was correct. No, Moby had to be stalked. A bait had to be put to him, precisely, individually, if I was going to cheat his smaller neighbours. Fortunately the river was clear and I could see what I was doing. Also there was plenty of cover to use but there my advantages ended.

I soon found that Moby would leave the cover of his raft and expect the first bait that was drifted near him. But once that first cast was refused then all further attempts – even with different baits – were totally ignored. It was as if Moby knew that an angler had moved in and it would pay him to lie low under his cover of green.

It was clear that my next step should be to anchor a bait close to the raft rather than fish it on the move. This is how ninety-five per cent of Norfolk chub men

BRAIDED LINE

Imagine you are fishing a swim on a river that you have been prebaiting for some while for chub or barbel. The light is closing in and you are expecting the fish soon to be on the move. After about half an hour the quivertip registers a strange, trembling bite. Perhaps you decide to strike or simply to let things develop. Either way, when you reel in you find that the hook and a couple of inches of line are missing. Examine the end of the line and you will most likely find that it has been cut clean through, although possibly depressed into more of an oval shape than a round one. What has happened? In all probability the fish, grown accustomed to the prebait, has taken the bait, swallowed it on the spot and its throat teeth have mashed both food and line.

If this happens more than once, you have probably got something of a problem on your

hands. One partial answer is to use braided line rather than nylon monofilament as a hooklink. Braid is far more difficult for fish to chew through and is far more resistant to even the sharpest of throat teeth. The other solution might be to fish the bait on some kind of bolt rig, perhaps with the feeder fixed some 6–9in from the hook. This sounds crude but the fish will probably feel the weight of the feeder and then bolt when it picks up the bait to give a positive bite for you to strike at before the throat teeth can come into play.

You might think that bite-offs are uncommon, but at certain times of the year there are swims where two or three can happen in a single session. Barbel are the main culprits, but, whatever the species, the consequences for the fish are more serious than is the dashing of our hopes.

Above: Two good chub work upstream, tipping up to take food from the gravel bottom. Though they are feeding hard, they can still be very hard to catch, as they are well aware of what is going on around them. The gin-clear water certainly gives them every chance to see terminal tackle or a bait that is presented badly.

Right: Chub will often tuck themselves in behind tufts of weed, and remain there for quite some time, all but invisible, before setting off to feed again as hunger dictates. When you spot fish like this, it often pays to trundle a bait close to them, just skirting the weed. If you can slow your bait down and stop it close to them it is very likely to be taken immediately.

This is the swim where 'Moby' lived for quite some time. On the left the alder virtually touches the water, and in days gone by there was a raft here that proved a magnet for both chub and barbel. Even now many fish frequent the area and the tree is a major feature in this whole stretch of river.

fish, watching the quivertip, and it soon became apparent that Moby knew this. Every static bait left him totally unmoved. I might have legered a lump of rock for all the interest he paid when I fished on the bottom.

I came to realize that my first attempt with a moving bait had to be perfect in every way or that very session I could wish him good day and move downstream for a barbel. I began to concentrate on presenting a bait at the right depth, with the right speed of fall, at the same pace as the river and on hook and line that were as inconspicuous as possible. Away from the fish, I experimented again and again with bait after bait. Sometimes I used a float and other times I freelined. I tried all combinations of shot until at last I began to feel happy that I had the best set-up for that rate of flow for both particles and bigger baits. The next day I moved into the raft swim with my confidence high. A big bait was my opening approach – a huge scoop of breadflake moulded round a size 4 hook that would take in water and bounce the gravels under his very nose. It trundled towards him. He cocked an eye when a four-pounder appeared from nowhere, scoffed the

lot and put an end to that opening gambit.

Next day I returned with a couple of pounds of corn and a different plan altogether. For an hour I fed in the loose grains until I turned the water before me into a mass of surging, heaving chub. The three and four-pounders I had fighting for feed by my bank while Moby stayed under the raft opposite, coming out now and again when I put two or three yellow grains down his side. Everything was set: the smaller fish were busy and lured away and Moby was interested and all alone. I felt I was close to a conclusion.

I changed from conventional line to 6lb copolymer. Perfect. A size 14 hook was very deep in a grain of corn, a number 6 shot was put six inches up the line, and I completed the outfit with a tiny quill set for three feet. I knew I would have just one chance. An under-arm flick and the bait landed dead in line to knock at Moby's very front door. I steered it to him. At a distance of four feet, the big chub saw the bait and stiffened. Two feet and he came into open water to watch. A foot now and he came up to intercept. Nine inches, six inches, a nose length, and then a confident gulp and Moby was pulling my line like Ahab's whale.

I lost him. It was either keep him from that raft or say goodbye. The line held, the knots took it all but the hook came back as straight as a needle. Like Moby of old, the chub had flicked his tail and was gone and I was left pondering a harsh lesson indeed.

142

CADDIS FLIES

Everybody knows that natural baits work for most British fish species but there is one that is rarely used here that really can be dynamite. I met up with the caddis larva in France, where maggots are very expensive and anglers use alternatives – often.

The caddis, or sedgefly, is a large insect not unlike a moth. However, it is as larvae that the angler is really interested in the insect. These live in tubes made of grains of sand or small pieces of twigs, leaves, shells or other material. The tubes are constructed in the first place out of a silk web made up of little threads which the larvae dribble out from the glands in their mouth.

The silky tube is sticky and easily fastens onto particles of material which the larva selects. The particles are not chosen at random and most species tend to use specific materials. For example, silverhorns use sand grains while great red sedges collect pieces of plant matter. Other species use small snail shells or pieces of gravel which help provide an excellent camouflage, so much so that many larvae are very difficult to see unless they are actually on the move. The tubes also act as a protection against predators and, being quite heavy, will help the light larva put weight on, fight the current and stay firmly anchored on the bottom where they want to be.

And that is where the French find them – under stones, half bricks and suchlike, in fairly fast, shallowish, clear water. Half an hour's hunting should produce enough caddis larva for quite an outing. Most will be stuck on the underneath of stones as you lift them out of the water and they are easily removed and popped into a bait container holding a little water. The baits are best removed from their tube by just pulling the material apart, nipping the grub and pulling it out intact. The grub will generally be about half an inch in length, and is best fished either singly or in little groups on good hooks for barbel, chub or roach.

In this type of water you will find all manner of bullheads, loach, crayfish and caddis lurking.

WHEN CHUB ARE DUFFERS

There was a well-known bridge pool which was home to a notorious chub of at least 5lb. Most of the anglers in the know had tried for him at some time or another over a season and a half, but there was nothing doing. The water was usually clear and the chub was quite aware when a car pulled up rather than passed over the bridge. He was one of those highly intelligent chub who are completely tuned in to everything the angler might choose to try.

My friend, however, had different ideas. Some way upstream, where the water was a little quicker and perhaps a little purer, he rummaged under some brickwork in a feeder stream and eventually managed to catch a bullhead, which he rejected, and two crayfish of about half an inch to 2in in length.

Taking care to keep his fingers from its rather nasty pincer-like claws, my friend hooked the bigger of the crayfish neatly through the tail onto a size 6 hook, pinched one swan shot 12in up the line and lobbed it a yard or so upstream from where he could see the chub working against the current.

Almost certainly the fish could see him, because he was just that sort of chub, with eyes that seemed to cover all 360 degrees. Perhaps he even saw the line as well for he had always done so in the past. Yet clearly that did not stop him now, for the sight of that crayfish jigging up and down before him, desperate to reach the safety of a piece of sunken brickwork, simply drove him wild. There was a spurt, an explosive take and there he was: a specimen of 5lb 2oz.

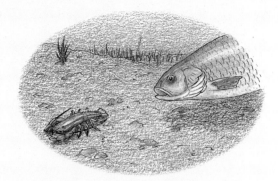

It has been recognized for a long time that chub adore crayfish and go crazy at the sight of them. They give huge, thumping bites as a result of their excitement but also because they are trying to kill the fish as quickly as possible to prevent it escaping. Sadly, however, nowadays crayfish should not be used as bait because they are scarce in most rivers. Always bear in mind that the waterside as a whole should be treated with respect and never plundered for short-term gain.

The obvious lesson was that while chub will reject every artificial and natural bait (even the juiciest of morning slugs), it seems that they just cannot ignore a crayfish. Now, after nearly two decades of further observation, I can state with confidence that chub have a fatal passion for them. But why? More than a favourite food, crayfish seem to be an obsession with chub. In fact I can think of only one other species that shares this desperate vulnerability, and that is the trout when mayflies are rising in the late spring – the brief period that game fishermen call 'duffers' fortnight'.

A wise angler investigates the shallow, rocky water just underneath a bridge for all manner of natural bait. We live in a world increasingly geared to convenience and most anglers are quite content to buy ready-packed baits from the tackle shop. Big fish are now familiar with these offerings and frequently reject them in favour of foods that are both much tastier and spell less danger.

On a food-rich river like this, roach often grow exceptionally large.

ROACH RHYTHMS

The fishing detective soon realizes that all species of fish are creatures of habit. River roach take this adherence to routine to extremes, and close observation will reveal that they move to specific areas at different times of the year. For example, in winter they tend to congregate in deeper, slower water, perhaps upstream of a mill. As spring and spawning time approach, they will move upstream towards shallower, quicker, rockier water. Very often roach will go back to the same spawning areas every year throughout their lives and it is not unusual, when the water is clear enough, to be able to recognize individual fish from one year to the next.

Feeding areas of shoaling roach

More vitally for the detective, roach shoals tend to like to feed in the same areas day after day. Many southern and eastern rivers are now over-enriched by agricultural run-off and in many cases a cloak of blanket weed is created over the bottom, hiding the gravels and chalk runs. However, there are places along every river where this weed is thin and if you look carefully when the water is low, there will be places where it is entirely absent.

These gleaming areas of gravel set amid huge swathes of blanket weed are almost always the places to which passing roach shoals go down to feed. In a mile of river it is not unusual to find patches of cleared sand, gravel or chalk, for example, every 60–80 yards, and if you watch a roach shoal it is in such places that they will linger the longest. If the clearing is sizeable, a shoal of roach might actually hang around it for several hours or even days. Every fishing detective knows this: when trying to locate roach on a river they simply look for those areas where blanket weed is at its thinnest or completely absent. Naturally this applies to the summer and the autumn, for in the winter the weed tends to die off and the water is often too coloured to allow any observation at all.

(Incidentally, dying blanket weed is an absolute nightmare to the angler trying to leger a bait. This despicable stuff rolls along the bottom, catches the line and builds up into sticky balls that clog the rod rings virtually every cast. It is extremely difficult to avoid this menace and the only remedy – and that a partial one – is to fish with as short a line as is practical.)

Once these areas clear of blanket weed have been located it makes sense (if you can get to the river fairly frequently) to prebait them as regularly as possible before fishing. The more often a roach shoal passes along and finds food the better. They will even begin to look specifically for introduced bait. In fact, if enough food is put in, even the shyest of big roach will soon settle into the rhythm and become catchable.

One of the best baits to introduce beforehand is bread: it is quite visible to fish and will remain attractive for several days. Also, it is less attractive to eels than maggots or casters are and, being slightly heavier, is less likely to be washed away in the current. (Another drawback of maggots is that they crawl under stones and becoming totally hidden.)

The other bonus of using bread is that it is highly vis-

Left: This is a famous roach stretch on the River Wensum at Bintree Mill. Just in front of the mill you will notice that the dark green of the bottom is broken here and there by light patches of sand. In the evening the roach move onto these to feed hard, and in doing so keep them free of weed. In all probability, however, the patches were first created by grubbing swans.

Right: You will occasionally come across small leeches on the gills and bodies of roach. In my experience this sight is much more common in the winter than in the summer, perhaps because roach are less active in cold weather and the parasites can establish themselves more easily. Pike and carp likewise host parasites, probably because both species spend a good deal of time lying on the bottom when the temperature drops.

Left: This may not be a great shot of the roach behind the chub but it does prove that the two species are compatible – something many specialist anglers have denied. It also confirms my findings over the years that roach really do prefer to feed over a clean bottom. I will not say that you will never find them feeding over weed but it is very rare.

Below left: When roach are feeding energetically you will often catch sight of a twist of silvery gold as a good fish turns in the current. In this case I had fed quite a lot of maggots to the fish and this had brought them up from the bottom. This is not always a good idea, however, as a heavier bottom bait is more likely to behave more convincingly and stands a better chance of being taken in clear water.

ible from the bank. Feed bread into as many bare areas as possible and return the next day to see if it has been eaten overnight. If it has, replace it and see what happens over the next twenty-four hours. After a while you can build up a reliable picture of those swims where the bread is being regularly eaten and therefore where your best efforts will be directed. Always make sure that the swims are deep enough to stop swans and other birds filching the bread before the roach move in, for you can be sorely misled by the activities of hungry waterfowl if you are not careful. In fact, wherever possible prebait in the late evening and go back in the early morning and you will be fairly sure

CHASING SHADOWS

This is an observation about trout fishing, but of relevance to coarse-fish detection nonetheless. It was August, beside the River Barle, a shallow, crystal-clear trout and sometime salmon stream that runs off Exmoor. The sun was high and the water was almost invisible – as were the trout. Then, little by little, I began to realize that there were long, thin, black reflections on the sand and gravel that moved from side to side in the current. What I was seeing were not the trout themselves but rather their shadows cast by the overhead sun. When I focused very carefully I could just about

see the small fish near the surface, but they were almost invisible, unlike their reflections clearly outlined on the river bed.

Roach in particular are often spotted like this in clear water in hot weather. True, their camouflage is not as efficient as that of the trout but frequently it is their shadow that gives them away. Remember to look for any useful clues – not just the actual fish.

I defy you to see the fish here. Look instead at the shadow which is firmly imprinted on the bottom just right of the centre of the shot.

that roach, rather than our feathered friends, will have cleared up the free offerings.

Rhythm is the key to success. Locate the feeding areas and serve up the food as regularly as possible and the roach will soon respond. Harmonize your actions with theirs, and you have a good chance of making some excellent catches.

Swans are a constant menace for the roach angler wanting to prebait on shallow rivers. Water more than 4ft deep should be safe, however, as this is the limit swans can reach by tipping up and extending their neck as far as possible. It is amusing to watch them trying to reach bait on the bottom that is just out of range. While this drives the poor creatures to distraction, it cannot be worse than our frustration when we see them eating a carefully laid bait!

FISH AND SEWAGE OUTFALLS

From our point of view it is difficult to understand why a sewage outfall should be so enticing to fish, for these are places that we shun. On most British waters, the disposal of sewage and other waste is tightly controlled, but it is surprising how much more frequently in Europe untreated effluent is pumped straight into rivers. Fish there, and here, are attracted to these areas largely because of the various items of food that come their way. Unappealing as it seems, it is possible to see roach, chub, barbel and even trout feeding happily from a stream of putrid water. I suppose that in summer the outfall can also provide cooler water, especially in Europe, where temperatures are more likely to soar. Equally, in the winter when temperatures have plummeted, such an area can often raise temperatures a little.

So, food and relief from extreme water temperatures seem to pull fish towards any type of outfall that we would automatically regard as unpleasant. Niffy as these areas frequently are,

the price of ignoring them is missed fish.

It does do to be very careful when fishing near outfalls, however. Obviously, if you were to be cut, an anti-tetanus injection could be called for. Also, as rats are frequently attracted to these places after dark, it pays to pack up as soon as the sun begins to set.

Inevitably most sewage outfalls are in built-up areas, but you will find them in the countryside too. Here the water carries a white tide of refuse off into the distance. The fish, however, were closely concentrated in the path of the sewage and proved surprisingly easy to catch on maggots, worms and flake trotted close to the bottom. Areas like this frequently repel the angler but prove very tempting to the fish. I remember, for example, Ireland's famous Slaughter House swim, where steaming blood from a bacon factory was tipped into the River Blackwater. The place absolutely stank of death and brine but the roach adored it and congregated there in their thousands. Admittedly not to everyone's taste, the only bait that worked was a globule of congealing blood wrapped around a size 12 hook!

A BRIDGE STRATEGY

There are times in detection when you have to think about more than just the fish and their habits, and logistics come into play very decisively. Let us look at the example of some barbel that positioned themselves, beneath a bridge, exactly midway across the River Wye at one of its widest points. There was no way that baiting would bring them closer in to either bank and the current was too strong to allow the delicate presentation that they demanded. It seemed to be a stalemate even though they could be seen feeding from the bridge parapet some thirty feet above the surface of the river.

It became increasingly obvious that the only way to put a bait to these barbel was to present it from the bridge itself. That way only a few feet of line would be in the water and I would even be able to see the bait in the water. In fact I had no doubt that I would hook barbel; the question was whether or not they could be

Above: Here we are on that bridge again and I am just throwing a rod down into the nettle patch beneath.

Left: I'm on the move, with a grin on my face as I cannot take the whole thing too seriously.

Above right: At last, a very nice fish indeed. If you look into the background, just above the fish's head, you will see the second arch and it was there the fish were lying, refusing to come any closer either side of the river. The water was quite high and coloured and rubbish coming down kept sweeping into my line and pulling the bait off course if I tried to fish from the bank. As it turned out, the overhanging approach was the only one that stood a chance of working that day.

landed. As I looked around me and thought carefully, a plan began to evolve and I decided to take the risk and try to hook a fish.

The first part worked extraordinarily well and within five minutes of starting to fish a fine barbel of around 5lb emerged from the rest, moved a couple of feet towards the bait and took it with no hesitation at all. I struck almost directly above the fish and the rod at once formed a gratifying curve.

The first move of the hooked barbel was to try and power underneath me, upstream, under the bridge itself. Not a good sign, but soon I turned it and, as I expected, it began to run off downstream into the pool itself. For three or four minutes I played it out very easily from my high vantage point. It was exciting to see the gyrations of the fish as it sought to shed the hook and find sanctuary. I walked along the bridge, leading it like a dog on a chain towards the bank. It was now wallowing now on the surface in the slack some

four yards out: now the action became intense.

Beneath the bridge, some five yards from the bank, grew a big clump of nettles. I simply dropped the rod into these so that it was cushioned as it hit the ground and as the rod was in mid air ran along the bridge, leapt the stile and shot down to the bank where the rod was lying. The line was tightening as the barbel was beginning to appreciate the slack and move back towards midstream. However, I was easily in time, the rod was quite intact and the barbel was brought back to the net, protesting feebly.

Altogether that day I caught four barbel in this way and lost not a single one. In fact, there was probably less danger of losing a fish than in approaching them from the bank, for the pressure from directly overhead made it impossible for them to reach any snags. Apart from enjoying the sport itself, it was gratifying to know that a one hundred per cent landing rate is unusual for big fish like these from such a wild river.

THE WARY DACE

I have a theory about big dace and why they are so difficult to catch on many rivers. It goes like this. Little fish are spawned, hatched and brought up in fast-flowing water. You can see them there on virtually any river, small, quicksilver fish like needles of light. They feed on passing nymphs, or even dry flies, and all their young life is spent developing keen eyesight and picking off quick-moving food. As a result, dace soon begin to develop a great awareness of the world around them and this makes it easy for them to spot any food that is behaving in a suspicious manner.

Big dace in clear water

By three or four years of age dace are masters at picking out a 'wrong 'un'. Around about their fifth or sixth year they tend to drop back in the water and frequent slightly slower, deeper reaches of the river. By this time they are big fish for the species, probably around 8–12oz, and they still possess the sharp eyesight of youth but now the water speed around them gives

them even more time to inspect a bait and reject it at will. And very often this is just what happens, so that a big dace in slow, clear water can be one of the hardest fish of all to catch.

However, days and weeks of watching and experimenting have provided me with a few tricks with which to bring about their downfall. Obviously you can fish with a bait anchored on the bottom and this will work at last light or at times well into darkness. The problem is that it is not a selective method and often the dace that you catch will not be the best of the shoal and frequently a stray, unwanted chub or roach will come along and spoil the whole situation. In many ways, then, I find it preferable to fish for these big dace during the day, when you can often see them and pick out the one you want. In such cases a moving bait of some sort will almost certainly be necessary.

Probably your very best chance will be your very first cast with a maggot, a caster or a piece of bread pinched on a small hook and fished with fine line so

Left: A perfect swim for small dace: water some 4ft deep flows swiftly over shingle and larger stones.

Below: Some nice dace cruise backwards and forwards over water cabbages – vegetation also favoured by roach.

Left: Sometimes it is very difficult to see through the surface of a river. Ripples caused by the wind or currents can disturb the surface so that what is happening below is completely obscured. However, if the wind drops or the current suddenly ceases, a 'window' on the water opens up and the fish are suddenly, if momentarily, visible. It is easy to understand the first, but if you have not seen the second phenomenon it may be difficult to picture the current ceasing abruptly. The fact is that a river is like a living thing and does not always progress in a predictable fashion. Sometimes there are strong pushes of water and then a momentary relaxation of the flow. It is in these quieter moments that the surface loses its wrinkles and the river briefly reveals the mysteries that lie below.

Right: Half a mile downstream from the dace swim in the photograph on page 154, the river slows dramatically and deepens to an average of 7–8ft. This is where the big dace show up – not often but enough to make fishing for them a possibility. The wildlife is a further attraction: in addition to the ducks which are causing an explosion of silver halfway down the picture, there are one or two little arrows on the water. One of these has been made by a travelling otter that has hunted through the night and is now looking for sanctuary as the day comes up.

that it slowly sinks and drifts past the fish that you want. That first cast might just catch the fish off its guard and it could be tempted into making an instant but rash mistake. If the bait is not taken immediately, you have problems, for from that point onwards the dace will look more and more warily at every successive cast.

If there are enough large dace in the shoal you might well be able to encourage competition by feeding in lots of maggots or whatever the bait is that you are using. The aim is to really stimulate the fish into a feeding orgy so that they give themselves less and less time to inspect food as it rains down around them. The hope is that two dace will descend on your bait at once, falling over themselves to eat it, and that one will take it in a rush. It must be said, however, that this does

not happen often.

Presuming it does not, what is probably your last chance is to stop feeding the swim and to leave it totally for five or six minutes. The dace will continue to mill round, looking for food and feeling hungry and frustrated. Then, put in the hookbait alone, without any free samples. It could well be that a fish will snap it up at once, worried that another shoal member will intercept it first. Also, with no free offerings to compare it with, the fish will find the hookbait that much more natural-looking.

Dace may be small but that does not mean they are not canny. If you want the very biggest specimens you really have to watch them, work out their ways and, crucially, never take them for granted.

Only a couple of acres in extent, this small irrigation pond is nevertheless a marvellously rich water where the constant variation in the level throughout the summer has produced a dynamic environment.

DETECTION IN STILLWATERS

STILLWATER CASE STUDIES

Detection is all about keeping an open mind, and using your ears, eyes and brain. Although in almost every fishing situation it is wrong to start off with rigid pre-conceptions, there are certain kinds of water that speak loud and clear to you at first sight.

Let's look at some common types of stillwater and consider what sort of clues they might provide. Large gravel pits are the biggest puzzle to many. They look so daunting, set in lunar landscapes with winds racing across them. New ones in particular are raw and unattractive, largely because there are few trees and little reed growth. Yet, as some of Britain's most specialist anglers have discovered, these waters can produce some of the most fantastic fishing that we in this country have ever witnessed.

Large pits

Unwelcoming as they may look, young pits are often particularly dynamic. For the first twelve or fifteen years they provide fantastic growth possibilities for all types of coarse fish even though this slows down in later years. A major reason for this early spurt is that the pioneering fish which settle in large pits at first suffer little competition and there is no danger of overstocking. Spawning is rarely very successful, for without tree growth around the margins and with water that tends to be too cold, reproduction is difficult. The fish stocks therefore tend to be low and as a result the individuals tend also to be large. As soon as there is a dependable rate of tree and weed growth, spawning becomes more successful and there are more fish,

more competition and average sizes begin to drop.

Large pits are generally very clear with luxuriant weeds that harbour in particular tench, bream and roach, although in many cases there is the occasional very large pike. Increasingly carp are stocked into these waters and because they do not breed here very often their average size can be immense. So, on a large, windswept pit expect the fishing to be difficult but if you are after specimens they could well be the kind of water to concentrate on.

Limited growth

Smaller, older gravel pits are often still clear but are frequently overgrown by trees. In all probability fish will have begun to spawn and the average weight of many fish may not be great. Tench, for example, will rarely exceed 5lb and roach and rudd might well be stunted. Pike are nearly always small and any high 'double' is an achievement. Carp, however, will often have been in the water for up to thirty or forty years, and these veterans can easily reach 35lb.

Sometimes bream can do well in such a water provided – and this vital – there are not many of them. If there is simply a group of three to ten fish, look out for large individuals. Old pits are generally beginning to silt up and this does aid spawning to a great extent and obviously puts pressure on foodstocks which are themselves waning as the pit ages. So, for anything but a big carp or the odd bream, it is probably best to look elsewhere for specimens – unless perch are your thing! Very often, especially if the roach and rudd are

Raw and uninviting on a still winter's day, this huge water is nevertheless the type of environment where big fish proliferate.

The bay of a large pit in France, purpose-built as a carp water. Notice how the bars have been left shallow to promote luxuriant weed growth.

This pit may be old and overgrown, but the water is still very rich in natural life.

Above: Now virtually a sanctuary, this pit has benefited from the fact that the farmers have stopped spraying round it. As a result, the wildflowers are growing extravagantly and in addition the water is becoming far cleaner and the average size of the fish is increasing.

prolific but small, perch can really accelerate in growth. Naturally, the same goes for eels.

In many country areas you will find clay and marl pits dug some way from villages in the middle of fields. Small waters almost always less than two acres, these have often been in existence for many years, and in some cases since the great agricultural changes of the eighteenth century. Usually the water in these pits is cloudy, or even milky, and local species such as roach, rudd and crucian carp will be present. Occasionally, though, larger species of carp will have been stocked and they might even have reached the 20lb mark. As in small gravel pits, eels and perch will in all probability do better than anything else, although a water that gets very little attention may well yield a few surprises.

Despite heavy pressure on land within village and town boundaries the old common ponds still frequently remain. These are generally small, shallow and cloudy and hold local species like roach, tench and small carp. Nearly always you will find that such waters have been over-enriched by centuries of duck life and big fish will be a rarity, unless some perch have managed to thrive on small roach stocks.

The most beautiful of stillwaters are the lakes that were constructed in the grounds of stately homes in the past two centuries. Generally these estate lakes cover between two and five acres but they can be larger. They often work in a cyclical way: for example, for periods they might be heavily weeded and then for three or four years they will be barren. Equally, fish

Above right: A very good bag of big eels, photographed as quickly as possible on a wet carp sack. Often the key to finding big eels is to try waters where eel-netters have not worked. These netsmen reckon they are about ninety-five percent effective, and although eels can often take twenty or thirty years to grow large, the chances of a big one are very remote if the water is netted every five years.

Right: No fishing detective gets very far unless he can move silently. Dabchicks are among the most timid of birds yet here one has come to within inches of my feet, seemingly oblivious of me and diving down to pick up pieces of sweetcorn that have dropped into the water from my catapult.

Left: A typical farm pond is small, shallow and with water like pea soup, but may well be home to some fair-sized carp.

Right: The lake at Blickling Hall in Norfolk is one of the most dynamic estate waters in the country. Despite the fact that it holds great numbers of fish, it continues to produce big bream, tench, carp and perch, and also a few 30lb pike. Part of the success of the lake may be explained by the fact it is built over chalk and as a result the water is crystal-clear and very rich in all manner of microscopic life.

Right: We tend to think of reservoirs as lowland creations, whereas they can be situated at quite high levels and still produce excellent fishing. This two-hundred-acre water lies at over 400ft in the Black Mountains in south Wales. All types of coarse fish grow to a large size there.

might grow very large, peak and then die off, to be replaced by a different species. It is most likely that originally tench, rudd, bream and perhaps (fully scaled) carp were stocked into these lakes, along with a few pike and perch. It is still possible that the descendants of these original introductions are alive and making good progress. However, estate lakes can be spoiled if they suffer from too much agricultural chemical run-off or, indeed, if large numbers of alien mirror carp are stocked. These will inevitably restrict the growth and

even threaten the very existence of more gentle species like rudd.

Irrigation reservoirs for agricultural use are a fairly new development. They are generally quite small waters that can provide a very rich environment. A major reason for this is the fact that the water level fluctuates wildly. The water may be high in April, for example, when the fish are spawning. However, by May or June the level may have dropped considerably as the water has been used on crops. As a result the

eggs may now be left high and dry on mud banks and will not hatch out. In this way spawning is often kept to a minimum and competition for food is not great.

When the water level drops, insects tend to colonize the bare banks and lay countless millions of eggs, and when it rises again these provide lavish foodstocks for the remaining fish. All this leads to a population of fewer but bigger fish. It is interesting that many irrigation reservoirs are built on the flood plains of rivers. In consequence, river species like chub can enter on occasion, and these will often do very well, especially if there are enough small fish for them to feed on.

Probably the most exciting sport for the big-fish specialist is that offered by reservoirs. These are huge environments which offer almost unlimited food supplies. Also, because they tend to be fairly cool spawning is restricted. Here again is that magic equation of low fish stocks and high food levels. As a result of these factors, reservoirs are ideal habitats for big tench,

bream, roach and pike. In some cases carp have been introduced, and because there is almost no chance of them spawning successfully in Britain, they tend to grow very large in size without increasing their numbers at all. However, finding them can be a major problem – as it can be for all the other species – because of the vastness of most of these waters.

We have looked at some useful clues that different kinds of stillwater offer us, but at the same time bear in mind that because every water is different you should always investigate a new venue with an open mind. Remember too that waters are never static and change dramatically from one year to the next. So never write off a water, saying that its tench, for example, are only average, for they can easily put on a couple of pounds over three or four years and you could be missing out on a bonanza. The most sensible approach is to visit stillwaters on your patch often and monitor them systematically each season.

Left: This relatively small estate lake was built around the turn of the century. It started life as home to bream and roach, but carp were stocked in the 1950s and the original occupants were netted out. Waters often contain fewer fish than people would like to believe, and as an illustration of this it took only a couple of netting sessions to remove the bream and roach. The populations that remained were never large enough to re-establish themselves and as a result gradually died out.

Above: This is a very rare sight today, especially on stillwaters. The photograph was taken on coastal marshes, where otters have more room to manoeuvre and more fish to feed on. Eels are a favourite item on the otter's menu and East Anglia's coastal dykes are full of them as they travel between there and the sea.

BODY TALK

Several divers of my acquaintance have noticed that whenever they go down in daylight they find eels pressed into the most inaccessible places and that often only their heads, if anything at all, are visible. Favourite spots are under the tangled roots of trees that crowd round islands or under boulders or amid fallen stone or brickwork. Certainly, the scientist Moriarty concluded from his researches that eels actually welcome the feel of a solid material pressing against their bodies. Whether this is simply to do with security or something more mysterious I would not like to say. Whatever the reason, the fact remains, and if you are looking for eels, especially in daylight before they begin to roam at dusk, it pays to position a bait hard up against any quite obvious snag-ridden area.

Just before his death, John Sidley, the great eel man of our times, talked to me on the phone about this particular characteristic of his favourite species. In fact, that coming summer, he told me, he was going to build eel 'homes' of his own so that he knew exactly where to place his baits. If I remember correctly, what he had in mind was to sink sections of piping that would fit a big eel like a glove. Sadly, John never lived to carry out this experiment, but perhaps someone will honour his name by testing out the idea.

DAPHNIA DAYS

It is mid to late summer and the weather has been warm for some time. As you look into the stillwater or very slow river you see a vast swathe of tiny rust-red or green particles shimmering in the light. What you are looking at is a vast concentration of zooplankton or tiny aquatic food forms such as water fleas, especially daphnia.

If you look very carefully you might spot roach, carp of all species, tench and bream drifting, apparently aimlessly, through this clouded water. They are taking in the food that nature has offered them. They are not like whales, which have gill-rakers and can sift out the organisms as they swallow and dispel the water. Instead they suck in and select the largest of the daphnia to swallow. Roach and carp, for example, are often extremely efficient at this, selecting up to a hundred large items of daphnia in a single minute.

When fish are feeding like this they are almost certainly preoccupied with very small food items, with the result that boilies or large pieces of flake, for example, are very likely to lie unheeded on the bottom. Even sweetcorn is alien to the range of foods that the fish are involved with. Now is the time for very small particles indeed, such as hempseed or squats (the smallest kind of maggot used as a hookbait). Fish can be caught when they are feeding on daphnia, but it is important to scale down and to imitate nature as closely as you can.

What the summer is all about — corn, poppies and a lovely fish from an almost unfished water where the tench are still happy to take large, unbalanced baits.

Crucian carp have come right to the surface of a large lake where the wind has blown great banks of daphnia into a small bay. Altogether eighty to a hundred crucians took part in this orgy of feeding. Despite this abundance of natural food, one or two fell for a tiny maggot on a size 20 hook suspended a couple of inches under the surface on a greased hooklength.

THE DAY OF THE TENCH

The year was 1987 and Roger Miller, my companion for the day, and I were fishing an estate lake for tench. The water was absolutely gin-clear – just as I like it for detective work. The sun, too, was just right and from 6am we could see everything that was happening in the water in front of us.

Feeding over hard bottoms

We knew from previous experience that the swim held quite a lot of tench and so that particular morning we decided to pile in a mass of bait. The swim was a sound one, with a very hard, sandy bottom, and set amid extensive blanket weed. There was no doubt that it had been enlarged by the burrowing of the tench and now was about the size of a normal kitchen, quite large enough for us both to fish side by side.

We fished quite traditionally with small baits like maggots, casters and sweetcorn on quite sensitive float tackle. Into the swim we threw small offerings mixed with hemp and by ten o'clock we had between forty-five and fifty tench feeding vigorously a rod's length in front of us. It was an amazing sight, and one I will never forget. Some of them were big, certainly

At times tench love to squeeze in and out of massed roots and weed. This fish lingered for ages, largely hidden by snags. But it was certainly feeding and a trickle of maggots soon attracted it and it followed them into the weedy area at the bottom of the lake.

seven and eight-pounders and as far as I could see there were none under 4 or 5lb. The amount of food they consumed was absolutely enormous and soon we had put virtually a gallon of bait in for them.

Now, all this was very gripping and nerve-racking. At first, that is, for the one problem was that by half past ten neither of us had had a single bite! Not once had the float as much as dipped even though every cast saw dozens of tench feeding round the bait and over the bait and doing everything to the bait except eating it. By eleven o'clock, even though the tench continued to feed madly we had stopped holding our rods or standing by them. We were just leaning against trees, bemused and, in the end, quite defeated – so much so that a little after eleven we left a swim that was still boiling with fish to go and visit another lake close by. Never has a detective been more defective!

Close-range observation

But I was not content to let the situation rest there and the next day I went back to the same swim and tried again, this time alone and determined to watch and see exactly what was happening, for there was no doubt that the food was being consumed. Before long I had managed to get the tench feeding right at my feet in water that was so shallow that I could have touched them. I had simply lobbed a bait out and crept to the bank, Polaroids on, and watched.

Now, remember what I was saying about hard bot-

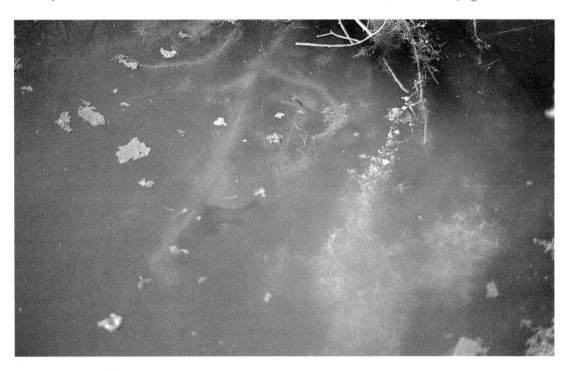

A good tench sails into view, as if suspended on the beams of sunlight…

It comes close into the bank and begins to dive as it sees food…

And finally dives to pick up food off the bottom.

Right: You should never keep tench in a net. They often find it difficult to orientate themselves and can easily turn over onto their backs or sides. Also, their mouths are very tender and sensitive and are easily harmed if they push against the mesh.

toms. These fish were cruising slowly one or two inches above the bottom of the lake and simply sucking food up from this distance. Maggots, hemp and even smaller grains of sweetcorn had no trouble lifting from the bottom and finding their way into the open mouths. However, the largest bits of sweetcorn and any bait with a hook in it simply stirred and rose a very little but not far enough to enter the fishes' mouths.

Clearly the fish were not frightened of the bait and avoiding it in any way, but rather it was simply that the bait with the hook inside could not rise into their open mouths, because it was too heavy. The point is that because the bottom was so clean the tench did not need to suck very vigorously to lift up their food: a little sip of breath was all that was needed. This all took place on a heavily fished water where most people used traditional big baits like pieces of breadflake and so it could have been that the tench also use this technique as a very effective defence mechanism.

Anyway, this was a perfect example of how detective work can be successful. It was a simple matter to return home and load pieces of sweetcorn with polystyrene so that just a little buoyancy was achieved, enough to counteract the weight of the hook. Success was pretty well immediate and next morning three or four tench were landed in just over a hour and a half before the rest of the shoal were spooked. Later experiments revealed that two or three floating casters on a size 16 hook would do just as well, but the point was that any bait that did not achieve neutral buoyancy with the hook in it could be almost certainly ruled out and discarded altogether. So, for big tench over hard bottoms subject to some angling pressure, detective work scored a notable victory.

Clear-water tench

Let's concentrate on big tench and think about how they behave and therefore how they can be caught. Tench are not an easy species to detect but there are opportunities, especially in the type of clear water that breeds big fish. And remember that is it big fish that we are talking about. Smaller, dirtier stillwaters rarely produce very big fish and there the tench grow lean and short, although they still possess grace, beauty and tremendous power. Clear-water fish, though, are something different and develop huge shoulders, deep flanks (even without spawn) and often have the most fabulously highlighted colours. In this connection let's look at a water where a useful piece of detective work occurred.

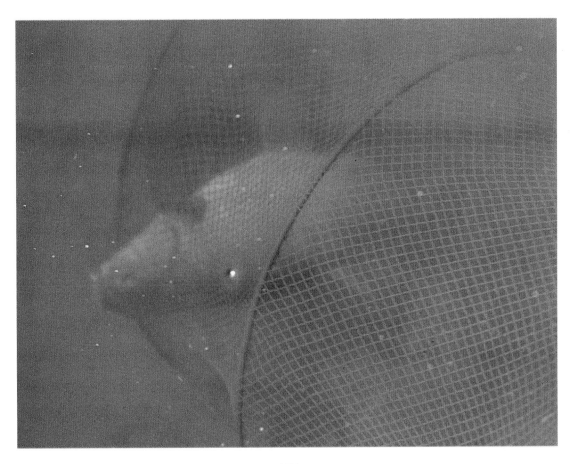

Left: Notice how this hard bank falls away into deeper water. This type of stony feature attracts tench and in the early morning they can be seen working their way along the lip between the shallows and deeper areas, feeding hard. A carpet of bait will almost certainly draw them down and the fishing can be quite fast and furious while each little group remains.

hard clay bottom

Above right and right: Tench love to feed over hard bottoms of clay, sand or gravel, but they do not really like silt at all. Over a hard bottom they have a distinctive preferred feeding action: they hover just above baits and at times suck them in from as close as a couple of inches. Naturally, they adopt a different approach when feeding over a silt bottom, otherwise they would suck up a lot of unwanted material with the food items.

tench hovers over bait and sucks it in from 1–2 inches

Below: Tight baiting and casting can be a great help. Here particles of food have been concentrated into a very restricted circle and tench have moved into the area. A sandy piece of water surrounded by quite thick weed growth, the swim was a good choice on their part.

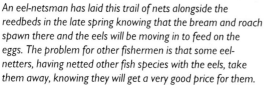

An eel-netsman has laid this trail of nets alongside the reedbeds in the late spring knowing that the bream and roach spawn there and the eels will be moving in to feed on the eggs. The problem for other fishermen is that some eel-netters, having netted other fish species with the eels, take them away, knowing they will get a very good price for them.

Large build-ups of surface weed are interesting in that they cut out the light and prevent the growth of aquatic weed beneath them. The tench appreciate both the shade that the floating weed gives and also the fact that the bottom below it is clean and suitable for browsing. Very often baits placed around the lip of floating weed can be very attractive.

In the early 1970s John Nunn, a well-known Norfolk angler and naturalist, lived on Sportsman's Broad and decided to tap into the eel harvest there in a small way and bought some fyke nets. Each May he laid these around the shoreline and very shortly made a surprising discovery: whenever he laid his nets along beds of bulrushes he caught tench in them as well as eels. Now this occurrence became an almost infallible rule and when our own tench fishing began in June not surprisingly we began to fish near to bulrushes.

Success was virtually instant and consistent, even though we had done little prebaiting, the water was large and the tench population was low. Simply by fishing close to these reedy landmarks we knew we would catch fish. There had to be a reason for this and at first we felt that the bulrushes were harbouring some type of insect on which tench like to feed. We even grubbed up quite a few and subjected them to a minute investigation, but there was nothing on the reeds themselves that could satisfactorily explain the phenomenon. Then one day, as the weather was warm, we decided to strip down to swimming trunks and investigate the areas around the bulrushes.

There was nothing particularly unusual apart from one thing: in the immediate vicinity of the bulrushes the bottom of the Broad was invariably hard, even stony. The only conclusion we could reach twenty years ago was that tench and hard bottoms somehow go together and that deduction has been reinforced on countless occasions since then. It really does seem that big tench in particular enjoy feeding, or certainly feed by preference, on areas where silt is at a minimum and food can be picked up in an almost hygienic way.

Welcome as this fortuitous discovery was, it was not without its problems, for although we knew more about the feeding habits of the tench, we now found that conventional methods of fishing for them were no longer effective, as I explain on page 176.

HEADS FLAT AND THIN

If you ever get the chance to study enough eels from enough different waters you will begin to realize that the shape of their heads can differ greatly, and that they seem to fall into one of two basic categories: the fat-headed and the thin-headed kinds. This phenomenon has been noticed by observant anglers over the last few years, as well by several scientists. It could be that the difference can be explained genetically – in other words, that there are two quite distinct subspecies. Fishing detectives, however, like to think otherwise.

It does seem to be something of a fact – and I stress the word something because here we are dealing of a minor mystery – that the thin-headed eels tend to live in lakes where there are not many small fish and the fat-headed eels inhabit lakes with plenty of such food items. It would seem that eels' prey is largely fry and fingerlings. The conclusion usually drawn from these facts is that thin-headed eels need greater dexterity to be able to survive by feeding on small foodstuffs such as snails, caddis, daphnia and the like. On the other hand, the fat-headed eels need bigger jaws and stronger teeth to grasp wriggling little roachlings.

It is always dangerous to reduce nature to cosy generalizations because you will always find exceptions to what is at best a shaky rule.

However, most people who have thought about this question admit that there is something in it. The practical application is that whichever kind of eel you catch you have at least got some sort of pointer to your best possible approach.

Let's say, for example, that the first eel you catch from a water has a narrow, tapering snout. What then? Well, the chances are that it is used to feeding on small foodstuffs and that you would do well to present it with a carpet of, say, maggots, casters or brandlings. The idea is that the eel will see a bed of small, wriggling baits and move in to gorge, eating enthusiastically until it comes across your own bait – three maggots presented on a strong size 12 hook, for example.

Conversely, if the first eel you catch has a large, broad head for its size and you know the lake is full of small fish, then it makes sense to fish with a bigger bait like a gudgeon, a small roach or two or three big lobworms. The chances are that these eels will want a more substantial mouthful.

One last point: it does not matter whether the eel is thin-headed or fat-headed – always strike as soon as you see a run develop. The old idea of waiting for the second run to begin was barbaric and generally resulted in a deep-hooked eel, and that means a dead eel.

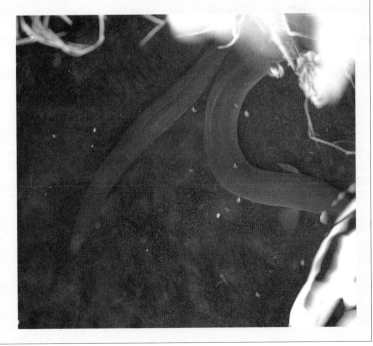

I can hardly believe my luck in getting this photograph, which was taken over the lip of a weir by pure chance. Both eels weighed about 4lb, but unusually one was of the narrow-headed type while the other was broad-headed. Neither was catchable on that day and both snaked off back into the brickwork of the mill once they became aware of my presence.

SHE

One fascinating thing about tench I learnt long ago was how deceptive the size of the fish in water could be. Tench that we thought would make 4lb in fact weighed 6lb and our imagined six-pounders easily became seven-pounders. You hear a lot about fish being magnified by water but really the opposite is true, especially in clear, deepish lakes. Anyway, the whole point of this observation is to introduce one particular female tench that I call 'She'. This fish was simply enormous, and even looked it in the water, so we dreaded to think how big she must have been on the bank. My estimate was around 9lb, but it was a conservative one and I liked to think that She was really quite a bit heavier than that!

A solitary specimen

Apart from her size, there were several other interesting things about She. The first was that by and large she tended to swim on her own. Now, any fishing detective will tell you that males generally congregate together, at least in the spring and during the early summer, as do the females. You will find males charging around in large groups, whereas the females drift on the margins of all this activity looking much more demure and graceful. She seemed to choose her own, generally solitary, route.

The second noticeable feature of She's behaviour was that she appeared to feed much later in the morning than the other tench. Most of them had passed their feeding peak by ten or eleven o'clock and that was often when She would make her first appearance.

Perhaps she had been feeding elsewhere in the lake, for her general demeanour was very placid and she took a great deal of time over any food pick-up. In fact, she would remain horizontal in the swim a foot from the bottom before tipping up, picking up one or two morsels and then chewing slowly. This activity could continue into the early afternoon and even dusk.

No fixed abode

Another thing that marked She out from the other fish was that she was particularly light in colour, much more so than any of the rest. Perhaps this had something to do with age. In addition, she tended to use far more of the lake than most of the other tench, which had recognizable patrol routes of two or three hundred yards. By contrast, She could often be seen either at the dam end or up in the shallows and it was as though this biggest of all the tench in that water had no real fixed abode at all.

I was in part motivated by the challenge of She and in part by the desire to vindicate my detective theory, but I was also curious to see just how big she would be. Now, let's look at the method we devised for big tench which, like She, live in clear, hard-bottomed

This is my one clear shot of what was, I am sure, the largest tench I have ever seen, and looking at her now I remember all her grace and quiet power. She was alone every time I saw her, although I suspect that originally she was part of a group of fish that died off over the years, thus accounting for her splendid isolation.

Differentiating between types of bubbles can often be very difficult and at first sight these bubbles could easily suggest carp or bream. It is only the shadowy form of the fish beneath that gives the culprit away as a tench. This aspect of detection is very important, as you will need to use different baits, tackle and methods according to the species of the bubbler.

waters. While semi-buoyant baits like maggots, casters and sweetcorn worked very well, the problem was that light tackle was needed.

Hooks could not be much larger than size 14 and if the line were much over 3–4lb breaking strain then bites would become impossible and generally 2–3lb line was necessary. The new copolymer lines that were at that time just coming onto the market made life a little easier and 4lb line could be used to the hook but it was still a pretty flimsy set-up for such a big fish in a large, weedy water and many of the fights were very lengthy. I dislike this approach for two reasons: first because it puts unnecessary strain on the fish which is unfair and second because the longer the fight the greater the risk there is of a hook slipping, the line fraying or a knot giving.

She came into the swim at around about 11.30 one morning, just when I was beginning to pack up my gear. She drifted in from the north and hung at the edge of the clearing, completely immobile, for some ten minutes. Then she dipped, picked up two grains of sweetcorn and resumed a horizontal position once more. By now the sun was very high and I could see absolutely everything that was happening.

Very cautiously I rebaited with a piece of poly-styrene-loaded corn and cast out way beyond her and gently retrieved the float so that it was about 18in in front of her nose. I could see the bait very clearly on the bottom. I had to leave it there for about an hour and a half before she moved right to the float itself and actually obscured my piece of corn. There the huge fish hung for ten minutes or so before, quite suddenly, tipping up. The float never moved, she returned to her horizontal position and the corn was no longer on the bottom. I struck.

A predictable outcome

This is not a book that describes great tussles featuring tortured rods and screaming reels; this has no place in observation and using your brain. But, believe me, the next fifteen minutes were pretty exciting! There was nothing I could do to move that big fish from the middle of the lake and she simply toured up and down pretty much as she fancied. I had never really felt such a big fish before, not at least on tackle that I knew was not up to the job. It was a humiliating experience and I was not surprised when eventually the hook pulled out, totally straightened.

Part of me was shattered to lose the fish that had been very much a target all summer, but at the same time I was surprisingly calm: I knew that I had not really deserved the fish and in fact felt I had rather tricked it into making a mistake on tackle that was not up to the job. The conclusion was simple: the buoyant baits and light tackle did work and detection had found a very vulnerable chink in the armour of these tench, although this could not be the whole answer to catching very big fish in snaggy waters.

LINE BITES

The line between water and rod tip tightens quickly, falls slack and then tightens again. The quivertip pulls round or the bobbin leaps. You tense. Should you strike? The line moves a little more firmly out and then quickly falls back limp. Again it happens after thirty or forty seconds and this time you hit it. Nothing!

Large fish in shallow water are always prone to giving line bites. This term is used to describe the line wrapping around the fin or looping over the fish's body. The problem is simply magnified with any shoal fish like bream or large roach, where there are far more fins for the line to become entangled with. With experience, line bites can be recognized by the frequent short lifts of the bite-indicator bobbin or jerks on the rod tip that end abruptly as the line slips off the fish's body.

Sometimes, the 'bite' will go on and on, but, of course, there is never a fish on the hook when you strike. Line bites can be very baffling but there are clues. For example, the bait is left untouched, or a fish rolls as you strike because the line pulling tight over his body startles him into trying to escape.

What can you do to lessen the impact and frustration of line bites? First, try to fish closer in. Clearly the less line there is in the water the less possibility there is of fish catching in it. Or try using a float rather than a leger, for if line is on the surface to the float there is less chance of fish catching it in midwater. If legering is a must, then try to sink your line totally on the bottom, for here again it is less likely to be fouled by passing fish. You can do this by really burying the rod tip right to the bottom after the cast and not drawing the line too tight when you lay the rod on the rests.

You have only got to watch fish that are giving line bites and being alarmed by false strikes to know how important it is to deal with the problem. A fish scared by line raking along its back is very likely to break up the shoal. Even a fruitless strike can split fish up and move them about as the bomb or swimfeeder moves through the shoal.

Typical of the kind of lake where you might expect line bites, this water is shallow and clear and you can just see the shapes of bream moving back and forth. This means that you need to fish at quite a distance. If you leger you will have a great deal of line in midwater and the chances of it being brushed against are very high. It is far better to float-fish with the line greased and lying on the surface all the way to the float or to leger with a sunken line on the bottom for as much of the way as possible. To achieve this, soak the line in a mixture of water and washing-up liquid and bury the rod tip well under the surface of the water, indeed almost to the bottom, so that the angle is less acute.

THINKING IT OUT

The loss of She was a milestone: obviously great strides had been made but it was still necessary to think of a way to get a buoyant bait into the tench's mouth on heavier gear. It did not take long to come up with the seemingly obvious solution of the hair-rig. Remember, all this took place a good few years ago and you will have to excuse the slow, plodding rate of this piece of detection!

Bit by bit we realized that 4 or 5lb line, and a size 14 hook, could be used with a small bait if this was attached to a hair. Maggots and casters were used but obviously corn is the favourite choice for the method. At first our hairs were too long and the tench simply sipped up the corn without taking the hook into its mouth. Bites were generally missed or if a tench connected with the hook it was generally outside the mouth. In the end, we found hairs of about half an inch worked best.

Keen-eyed tench

Hair-rigs breathed new life into the situation and the tench that were hooked were landed but soon it became apparent that fewer and fewer tench were making any mistakes in the first place. Observation again came in useful: two tench came over the swim (we were still fishing the hard-bottomed one). They

Two tench, swimming close together, move into the swim.

were clearly hungry and began to tip and eat until they came within two feet of the float and line leading to the bottom of the lake. They then fled! Over the next two weeks we noticed this more and more and even if the tench were not visibly panicked they began to sidle out of the area as soon as a float appeared. It is all too easy to underestimate the power of those little red eyes and clearly they see far more than we think.

At the same time something else happened: we began to realize that even free offerings of corn were being left in increasing amounts. Hemp remained a favourite and casters too were disappearing, but the corn was not. Obviously the bait was past its best. This led to a period of using casters, maggots or even hemp (which is very awkward on a hair) and again catches picked up for a while.

During the close season a new possibility emerged, one that is now widely accepted, but think how detection had moved me and my friends towards this conclusion. We wondered what would happen if, over hard-bottomed swims, we introduced baits that were quite heavy and needed a greater amount of suction from the tench to raise them into their mouths. That way we should be able to get decent bites on big baits that would make the whole operation much less fiddly. This method we put into practice the next season, using small boiled baits in quite large quantities.

Obviously these baits could be seen easily in the

Above: On occasion tench bubble furiously – quite as dramatically as carp. But here again the question of identification arises. In this case the culprit was a carp and one clue is that often the bubbles are further apart than when a tench is responsible. Also, the strings of bubbles from a carp tend to meander rather more quickly as the tench moves more slowly along the bottom. However, with bubbling there is never absolute certainty, and naturally it helps to see the fish itself.

Left: Tench are great browsers on daphnia and here one looms through the water towards a band of the tiny creatures. It is a mistake to think of tench as purely bottom feeders, and often a very small, slowly drifting bait will prove very acceptable.

gin-clear water and it was a while before the tench began to accept them freely as food. But once they did the action was intense, for the new foodstuffs had driven them into a near frenzy. And, we were right! These heavier baits that we had switched to gave the tench no option but to suck hard. It was possible to mount them on hooks as big as size 12 and still get quite positive bites – even though now we were forced to leger and lay all our line hard on the bottom.

In a way we had come round full circle to using large, heavy baits like the anglers around us who were still doggedly persevering with flake and big lobworms. Detection is a funny thing. You think you are making all sorts of advances only to arrive back at where you started, but at least we had learnt a lot on the way. And one thing is for sure: never again will I underestimate anything about the tench, who is very far from the rather dozy creature that many anglers think he is.

SCARLET AND GOLD

I was fishing a shallow estate lake one July day around noon, and the sun was streaming from a blue sky. The water, which was crystal-clear and about 4ft deep, shimmered over a sandy bottom punctuated by the occasional frond of weed. All in all, it was a glorious scene. All at once, sweeping from left to right across my vision, processed a shoal of rudd. I had never seen anything like it before and the memory will stay with me for ever. It was a carpet, a tapestry, of flickering gold and scarlet as the sun played off the brassy flanks and glowing fins. Like gold dust mixing with flame, it was an explosion of colour, and all the more so against that backdrop of blazing blues and greens.

The shoal was constantly on the move, rippling and shimmering like some fantasy, but then that is the very nature of rudd: never still, always wary, searching for food or safety.

Since that memorable day I have seen the sight repeated in Ireland, all through England and Europe and even as far afield as Kazakhstan. It was there, in a lagoon just off the Caspian Sea, that I most recently saw the scarlet and gold carpet. The fish were huge and accepted the fly that I cast to them. Again the sky was a brilliant blue, as though that scene from many years earlier was being re-enacted for me. It was one of those sights with which the observant angler is rewarded from time to time.

This beautiful country lake with spreads of lily pads is a classic rudd water. It has not been interfered with for at least seventy years and still maintains some original stocks of fish. The problem is that the rudd tend to overbreed and are generally quite small, although fish of 1lb or more turn up from time to time.

A QUESTION OF WIND

We are all familiar with those still days with clear skies when the water is really bright and there is little doing in the summer and the fishing is even worse in the winter. Conditions like this, especially after October and the leaf fall, tend to be the kiss of death for roach and bream especially. The only consolation is that things sometimes improve slightly at night when the light has gone from the sky and the fish slowly and reluctantly begin to move and feed. We all know, too, that windy days mean quite the reverse, especially when there are warm, wet skies and the water is clouded either through wind action or heavy rain. Then, whatever the season, the fish are much more likely to feed throughout the day.

For many years I thought that water temperature and clarity were pretty much all there was to consider on the large stillwaters. I was wrong. Trying a new style of fishing made me reconsider the situation. First of all I began to fish the Scottish lochs for pike and to appreciate the enormous amount of undertow that often builds up on waters of this size. In fact, I experienced underwater currents strong enough to pull a 2oz bomb along the bottom like a small split shot. My experiences in Scotland taught me to see the water in a three-dimensional way. As a result I began to see it as cross-sections layered with currents, as well as in terms of depths.

Secondly, I began to fish for roach on Ardleigh Reservoir in Essex. There I discovered the same type of thing, although to a slightly lesser degree. Here, at times, a 1oz bomb was quite easily bounced along the bottom. What emerged from my fishing at Ardleigh

Right: Note the large, completely flat area at the start of the ripple in the centre of the picture. This tell-tale sign has just been produced by a carp rolling under the surface. All good carp anglers spend a great deal of time scanning the surface of lakes, often with binoculars, for clues like this.

Below: The type of morning every angler dreads: a heavy frost after a still night and a lake that is frozen hard, as can be seen from the distant piece of timber resting on the ice. At such times there is no chance at all of fishing for a good few days.

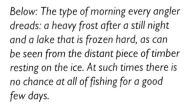

was quite simple. When there was, or had been, wind strong enough to set up an undertow, I caught fish. When I was not fishing in an undertow, I did not.

For a while at Ardleigh I was in the habit of setting up at a predetermined area. Sometimes there was a local undertow – and I caught roach – and sometimes there was not – and I caught nothing. As a result, I began to experiment with swims along the bank until I found an undertow, and then, almost always, roach appeared. Once an undertow subsided during the session there would be no more fish, and I had either to pack up or move swims until I found another.

Finding an undertow

How do you locate an undertow? There is no easy answer, for very often the areas in which you would expect to find one simply do not produce. Sometimes, although not always, the areas of a stillwater that are most effected by choppy waves have the strongest undertows. Areas of coloured water can also possess such currents. However, the best thing is to travel light, casting around with an empty swimfeeder and seeing if it holds bottom easily or moves a lot through the water. The more positively the swimfeeder bounces along the bottom then the stronger the undertow and the more likely you are to find roach.

But why do roach like undertows so much? Well, I can only guess that these underwater currents bring either food or fresher, better-oxygenated water along and that the fish like these. On the other hand, they may like the feel of moving water or perhaps undertows make them feel safer from predators. Perhaps we will never know for sure. In the meantime all we can do is use our eyes and our common sense to build up a better picture of fish behaviour.

THE FEEDING BREAM

It is a June evening after a warm day on the lake at Blickling Hall in Norfolk. You stand on the dam wall, looking south towards the great house, which is obscured by a high bank and trees. The wood behind you keeps away any breeze drifting in from the sea and the water is still enough to register the pin-prick tench bubbles ten yards out, drifting up through seven feet of water. Now and again, a tench actually rolls, absolutely silently, silhouetted against the pink and crimson water. Beautiful. The sweetest of clues to a feeding fish…

Patrol routes

The sun rapidly descends towards a tree line in the west. It is all but gone now, glowing like a lantern in the branches, when another fish rolls, further out, bigger, blacker, more noisily than the tench. Seconds later another fish shows and then a third almost immediately afterwards. From now until darkness forces you off the water, the bream shoal very slowly moves right to left along the wall in front of you. In the two hours you are there, watching, the fish progress only about a

hundred yards and even as you leave you can hear them splashing, out there in the blackness.

The next night reveals exactly the same thing. And the next. Were night fishing allowed at Blickling, then it would be the easiest thing in the world to put bait out where you now know the fish will come to and wait for the inevitable action to follow. But you are not allowed to fish there before the crack in the eastern sky next morning, four hours or so away.

It is 3.55am. There the bream are, at the extreme eastern side of the dam and even spreading a little way up the bank to the left as you look. During the hours you have been away the shoal has travelled a further hundred to one hundred and fifty yards. Now you know exactly where to put out bait this coming evening, at last light, so that the bream will find it and work there all the way through tomorrow's dawn. Why put the bait out at last light? Because then there is less chance of swans, ducks and other diving birds eating it. Who says the bream will follow the same routine? These patrol routes are pretty accurately adhered to day after day, week after week until the

Left: A large bream makes its typical bow-wave through the sleepy water around sunset.

Below left: This fast-moving, dark-bodied bream is clearly not feeding but has somehow become separated from its shoal and is almost certainly keen to rejoin it. A bait put to such a fish will almost invariably be rejected, no matter how temptingly displayed.

Right: The perfect bream angler's dawn: the water is just beginning to give off mist, which often stimulates the species into feeding.

It is very rare to see bream feed as close into the bank as these fish, especially on stillwaters, where they usually like to stay at least thirty yards out. What attracted these fish, I am not sure. However, over the previous few days a strong north-westerly wind had been blowing towards this bank, causing a great deal of coloured water in that locality. It might well have been that fish were still there, investigating, seeing what the storm had disturbed. Fishing small brandlings just beyond the rod tip paid off for one angler, but as the sun rose higher and the water became progressively clearer, the bream disappeared from view.

weather changes, supplies dry up or there is an explosion of food elsewhere on the lake.

Of course, this is not the only bream shoal on a water the size of Blickling – there are several more operating in several places around the lake. This is the way that many bream live, gently and predictably making it easy for the angler who puts in the time and uses his eyes to read the evidence they are only too keen, as it seems, to give away.

I have watched bream feeding from punts, from foot bridges and I have even swum with them when the water has been warm and clear and the bottom hard. There are three things that have struck me through the years. The first is their slow, steady way of feeding. They do not like to be rushed at all, and are very loath to change their feeding habits, unlike carp, say, which can get carried away with particularly attractive food sources.

Second, because the bream is generally a very deep, barrel-chested fish it has no option but to tip up to feed. Of course, all fish have to do this, but it is of necessity more marked in bream. Therefore a shoal of horizontal bream is simply not feeding, and you can see these groups of fish drifting around on many a hot day with food very far from their minds. However, if you see a shoal of vertical bream it is an odds-on probability that there will be bubbles, clouded water and heavily feeding fish.

Lastly, I think – I am still not entirely sure – that a bream holds a certain amount of food in its lips while it grazes vertically. It might move some way, searching for more titbits before righting itself to the horizontal and starting to chew. At the rod end you will see a bite register as soon as the bait is picked up in the lips. It is very tempting to strike immediately but probably all you will do in most cases is pull the bait from the bream's lips and startle that fish and possibly the entire shoal. The answer is to wait until the reel actually begins to revolve. This ensures as far as is possible that the bait is well into the bream's mouth and that the fish has righted itself.

Heavy or coarse terminal gear are not suitable for this approach, as the bream will feel resistance and spit the bait out very quickly. The best bet is a long hook-length of light line complemented by small hooks and small baits so that the bream will feel little unusual drag and sense nothing wrong until it is too late.

Above: Even though it is not very distinct, I value this shot because it shows the largest bream that I have ever photographed in the water: a fine specimen of 10lb 9oz. It was first seen in a large clear millpool, slowly working its way upstream and tipping to feed every now and again as it went. Here it is moving from the horizontal and going down onto the bed. Notice its massive shoulders, a clue to the weight. Maggots fished on a size 14 hook to 3lb line brought about its downfall.

Below: Carp, tench or bream? From the photographic evidence alone I would say that the culprits were carp or bream, because the bubbles are fiercer and more widespread than is usually the case with tench. In fact, I took the shot and I know which species was responsible – about six or seven bream feeding hard over a bed of groundbait.

THE WATCHER

Sometimes watching somebody fishing can be as instructive as watching the fish and their behaviour patterns. You see exactly how the fish react to baits and tackle and learn a great deal about actually catching them. I certainly understood much more about crucian carp after spending a few hours watching Bernie Neave in action at a local lake.

Before that day I felt I knew most of what there was to know about crucians, and certainly about the water in question, but I was mistaken. It was high summer and the day was very bright, and the water very low and clear, unusually so for that lake. I sat on a high bank behind Bernie and this gave me a perfect view of the water. I had absolutely no desire to fish – I was merely interested in studying Bernie's float, his bait and the reaction the crucians had to it.

The swim was about two and a half feet deep and Bernie was fishing to his right about twelve feet from the bank. A little further down a large willow tree overhung the water and in many ways this was to prove the key to what happened during the day. The first thing that was impossible to miss was the fact that the crucian carp were holed up under the willow, which provided a great deal of shade, and they quickly came out in little groups of four or six fish to feed in Bernie's baited area for around ten minutes before returning to the shade of the tree. It was difficult to make out individual fish but my own impressions were that there were thirty or forty crucians in the area, some of which would come out every half hour or so, establishing an easily recognizable feeding pattern.

Once the crucians reached the baited area they worked very slowly and very steadily, tipping up and feeding just like their larger true carp cousins or tench. There was no hurry whatsoever in any of their actions and it seemed that they were browsing the bottom in

Crucian carp are extraordinary fish and will at times feed at the surface, especially after dark. This happens far more often than most crucian anglers expect, although here a group of the fish are feeding in this way in broad daylight, which is not a particularly common sight.

A crucian swirls for floating bread. Soon afterwards it fell for a big piece of flake pinched on to a size 10 hook and allowed to drift down through the top foot of water.

THE SOFT TOUCH

It was a hot spring day and frog spawn lay thickly on the stems of the arrowhead lilies. Above was a high bank from which it was possible to see most of the water and sure enough, as I expected, the crucian carp were beginning to put in their first appearances of the year. Three or four fish virtually at my feet interested me greatly as they pushed their way through the arrowheads. I was not that surprised to see them eating the frog spawn slowly and deliberately but what was fascinating was the way that they sucked in globules only to blow them out again several times before finally swallowing each jelly-like piece. Each fish was eating in this manner and it reminded me of a time that I kept a pet crucian by my bed in a large tank with an eel, a perch and a baby rainbow trout.

The favourite food of all four proved to be tadpoles and the eel simply went crazy at the very sight. So did the crucian, in his own way: he would suck in a tadpole from an inch or more and blow it out again several times until the creature was dizzy and dying and then, pop, down it would go. He behaved in exactly this way with every foodstuff I offered him.

It is this behaviour that I am convinced makes crucian bites so infuriatingly difficult to hit. You see, they just suck and blow, again and again, making the float dither and dip, so that you never quite know when to hit it. What the crucians are doing, I am quite sure, is softening a bait up until it needs precious little chewing in the throat, and this is where I believe short cuts can be made.

These observations have for a long time led me to make baits for crucians as soft as possible. Breadflake, for example, I keep completely fluffy and just nip it to the shank in the hook. A wasp grub is a much better bait than a maggot because it is so soft-skinned and easily punctured. But best of all in my experience are small balls of paste made up from the groundbait itself. What I am sure happens is that the groundbait balls dissolve on the bottom and the hook simply lies amid a minute heap of particles. The crucian comes along and sucks them in and begins to swallow immediately. Very often the bite is extraordinarily positive and the crucian is hooked well into the mouth rather than on the outside of the lips as is so common with these extraordinary little carp.

Look carefully and you will see the head of a very large crucian carp just poking through the weed a third of the way up from the bottom of the photograph. Its mouth is pushed open, and it is voraciously sucking in tadpoles, shrimps, snails and water fleas. For an hour the fish hardly moved at all, simply turning round in the small hole it had made for itself, feeding hard.

What is the fish that you can see slinking away from the surface of this milky water? Answer: a large bream. At least I think so!

a vertical way, feeding for some thirty to forty-five seconds before straightening up again and chewing. Very often one fish would cover some two square feet in four or five minutes or so and then go back to the shade of the willow. On other occasions another tour or two of the bottom would take place. But never was there any rush – unless Bernie struck!

Line bites

Very frequently, crucians would be operating around Bernie's float but not over his bait and still the float would dither and duck. Presumably this was a result of their bodies or fins touching the line or even the wash as they passed it. If Bernie struck at any of these movements then his bait rose quite obviously from the bottom and the fish were immediately startled. Sometimes they would even sprint back to the security of the willow tree. But on other occasions they would simply stop feeding and move away two or three feet for a minute or two before returning and feeding again. On the occasions that Bernie struck and a crucian was hooked, all that fish's companions would leave the shelter of the willow and not be seen again for some while.

These observations reinforced a belief I had built up over the years that crucians are a very aware and very cautious breed of fish. It was rewarding to see this theory so dramatically confirmed.

A true monster

This story has an element of drama as well as instruction. The lake never produced what one would call a whopper, yielding crucians of an average weight of 1–1½lb, with the occasional fish of around the 2lb mark. Then I saw it! Towards the end of the session, from under the shade of the willow, glided the largest crucian I have ever seen in my life, before or since or even in my dreams. And the most amazing thing was that it simply moved straight under Bernie's float, tipped and sucked in the bait. Once hooked, that mighty crucian powered its way back to the willow and Bernie hung on, hung on and… lost it! He looked up and asked: 'A tench?' I shook my head. I could hardly bear to tell him what I had seen. Now, if there is a moral to this tale it must be that in any crucian pond the odd true monster can lurk and, believe me, that fish just had to be nearer 5lb than four!

That three-hour session watching a very good crucian angler taught me more about the species than I think I have ever picked up in many seasons of experience. Now I never fish away from shade and I never strike unless I am reasonably confident that I will be successful. And I always live in hope that a monster like Bernie's lost fish will be just below the next willow.

INDEX